Soci...
in

Social Studies in a Mass Society

edited by

DALE L. BRUBAKER

University of California, Santa Barbara

INTERNATIONAL TEXTBOOK COMPANY
Scranton, Pennsylvania

The International Series in

SECONDARY EDUCATION

Consulting Editor

JOHN E. SEARLES

Pennsylvania State University

Standard Book Number 7002 2200 6

To

COLE S. BREMBECK

Teacher, Scholar, and Friend

Foreword

Among the indictments leveled at the teaching of secondary school social studies in recent years, two of the most prominent have been that topics have not focused on the deepest concerns of our society nor have they provided students with serious intellectual challenge. If we may grant that these charges are well founded, at least in many schools, then the question becomes: What can be done about it?

I believe this book contains one promising answer. In a single volume Dr. Brubaker and his coauthors furnish teachers with insights into a variety of current areas of interest regarding American society—insights that should stimulate more effective teaching of the social studies.

Several chapters treat popular social problems as they relate to the schools: urban slum versus the affluent suburb, public schools and America's "two religions," mass media and politics. Others center on organizational structure in complex modern societies and on interpretations of "democratic" schools. Still other chapters illustrate unusual approaches to social studies: developing units around such concepts as national character and philosophy.

The chapters, when viewed from another perspective, can be divided into two general categories:

First are those which investigate social issues in the realms of religion, democratic education, organizational problems, urban conditions, and mass communication. Each of these topics is discussed from the viewpoint of the social scientist. Then the manner in which the concepts can be best pursued in the classroom is turned over to the teacher.

Second are the chapters which not only introduce uncommon topics of study but also describe in some detail instructional strategies which may be used in secondary school classrooms. In other words, the reader is provided descriptions of ways to teach topics like philosophy or comparative social studies so he may judge how well such approaches might suit his own students and his own teaching style.

In effect, Social Studies in a Mass Society displays a combination of virtues which should ensure it a favored position in contemporary social studies literature. It casts sound scholarship in interesting prose, examines problems of deep concern in American society, and promises high school students serious intellectual challenge.

R. MURRAY THOMAS
Santa Barbara, California

Preface

This book is written primarily for three groups of people, all of whom are interested in the social studies: (1) future social studies teachers; (2) social studies teachers now teaching; and (3) social studies educators, social scientists, and historians.

The future social studies teacher is anxious about tomorrow, his most recent contact with the schools probably being four or five years ago when he was a student in secondary school. His anxiety may be expressed in the many questions he asks: Have schools changed since I was a student? Will I be able to maintain some order in the classroom? What are today's students like? Has our society changed in the last few years? What problems will I face as a teacher? Will I be able to handle these problems? He wonders, in short, if he will be able to be a good teacher. Any teacher will admit that classroom management is necessary if learning is to occur. Yet much more than classroom management is important to good teaching. The teacher must be acquainted with recent developments in his subject matter field as well as various teaching methods designed to reach desired objectives. The teacher must also see that what his students learn will be part of the larger society in which they live. The chapters in this book are aimed at helping the student gain perspective on all of these matters. The Herculean nature of this task is obvious. This book is but a beginning effort toward an admirable goal.

Those social studies teachers now teaching have similar goals to those of the future social studies teachers. However, unlike the future teacher, the more seasoned teacher is not primarily concerned with classroom management and can instead center his attention on weighing various content and methods of teaching, always bearing in mind, of course, individual and group differences. How can I do a better job with my teaching? is the question foremost in his mind. In asking this question, he remembers specific problems yet unsolved and anticipates problems he may face in the future. How will I reach this group of slow learners? How will I organize my American history class so that the students will be more interested? How will what I teach my students be important to them when they graduate from high school? The experienced teacher is forced to place his teaching in the wider perspective of society as a whole. This book shares his concern for a wider view.

Social studies educators, social scientists, and historians are looked to for leadership by future teachers and those presently teaching the social studies. Post-Sputnik interest in mathematics and science has carried over to the social studies. Present ferment is indicative of the challenge and responsibility felt by university professors interested in social studies education. No individual or group has dominated the area of social studies so that many and diverse points of view are being heard. What should be the relationship between the humanities and the social sciences? Should the social studies be organized along disciplinary lines or are there effective ways in which the disciplines can be merged? What directions should research in the social studies take? What is the primary goal for social studies instruction? What methods and materials should be tried in a variety of teaching situations? How can the social studies more accurately reflect the larger society in which students will live upon graduation from high school? Answers to these questions may be discovered as we identify certain crucial areas in the social studies—areas to be explored in a more sophisticated way by individual studies. Such an identification and beginning efforts to answer previously raised questions are the aims of this book.

An annotated bibliography at the end of each chapter is included to encourage the reader to pursue each area in greater depth. Introductory summaries to each chapter are not included for it is the editor's belief that each chapter best speaks for itself in its entirety.

The editor wishes to express his appreciation to his colleagues at the University of California, Santa Barbara, for reading parts of the manuscript. Special appreciation is due to Professors Alan S. Katchen and R. Murray Thomas for their discerning comments and encouragement.

The editor owes a special debt of gratitude to Mrs. Cleo Dietz, Mrs. Dorothy Damewood, and Mrs. Ruth Keagy for typing the manuscript at various stages.

The staff of International Textbook Company and its Education Editor, John L. Dugan, Jr., were as usual most helpful in seeing the book through to its completion.

The book is dedicated to Professor Cole S. Brembeck for aid and encouragement through graduate school and beyond.

DALE L. BRUBAKER

Santa Barbara, California
January 1969

Contents

Introduction

During the last decade attention has been focused on the shortcomings of the social studies. Criticism has been levied at that which has been taught and at that which has been neglected. The result has been a mixture of optimism and fear, a desire to change and a reluctance to tread from the status quo. The position of the social studies teacher is an ambivalent one, for individuals and groups around the nation are trying to translate their interests and beliefs into programs which will influence students in social studies classes.

The areas discussed in this book are designated as crucial because criticism has been directed at them as they are presently being taught or as they are presently being neglected. The remainder of this introduction cites these criticisms and discusses how the following chapters have been written to suggest possible solutions to the present dilemma.

The Antiseptic Curriculum

One has only to examine social studies textbooks to realize that the suburban middle-class white child is the prototype for all students. This model is a world apart from the student who lives in our urban ghettos. Both the social studies students in the slums and suburbs suffer from the antiseptic nature of the social studies curriculum, according to Susan Lynn Jacoby in her chapter entitled "Slum and Suburb: The Neglected Reality." Her plea for commitment, backed up with knowledge and courage, challenges the reader to create a more realistic social studies curriculum.

The Avoidance of Controversy

Although the analysis of controversial subjects should be a major part of the social studies, such analysis is frequently missing for teachers are sensitive to the pressures of the social system in which they operate. The areas of religion and philosophy provide a special challenge to the social studies teacher. His acquaintance with recent legislation on such matters as prayers in school suggests prevailing interest and concern for the separation of church and state *and* the socialization of the student in a "proper" value system. It is precisely the relationship between religion and public education which is explored in Robert E. Michaelsen's chapter, "The Public Schools and 'America's Two Religions.'" Professor Michaelsen treats the major theses in this controversial area in historical perspective, and then suggests how greater clarity might be brought to future dialogue on the relationship between denominational religion and common-faith religion.

W. Eugene Hedley's chapter, "Philosophy and Inquiry", logically follows the chapter by Professor Michaelsen. Philosophers are tempted to ask for a separate course in Philosophy in the social studies curriculum. Professor Hedley suggests an exciting alternative to such a request. His emphasis on inquiry is very much in line with recent emphasis in the social studies on critical thinking.

Obsession With Structure at the Expense of Reality

Anyone who has had social studies courses remembers memorizing facts about the three branches of government. Social studies courses have consisted of a structural study of government at the expense of an understanding of the inner workings of institutions. As Robert G. Hanvey, Curriculum Research Director for the American Anthropological Association, has so aptly stated, "Bureaucratic behavior. . .is a problem of long-standing interest to sociologists, political scientists, and more recently to anthropologists. As a topic for study in the schools, color it missing."*

Why have social studies courses neglected reality and instead presented a superficial treatment of daily behavior? One reason is that we have felt compelled to rationalize our actions with a very idealized conception of "democracy". "Democracy" has for many been equated with a lack of control. We have, in short, been unable to give preciseness to our everyday use of terms.

Ronald E. Blood's chapter "Democratic Schools? or Schools in a Democracy" deals with the concept of democracy as used by administrators, teachers, and students in our schools. David P. Gardner deals with bureaucratic behavior in his chapter entitled "Organizations and Modern Society." It is hoped that these chapters will help fill the void cited by Robert G. Hanvey.

Simple Neglect

Some areas of the world outside the schools have simply been neglected. The mass media are a case in point. As with the study of bureaucracies, the

---

*Robert G. Hanvey, "Social Myth vs. Social Science," *Saturday Review*, November 18, 1967, pp. 80-81 and 94-95.

study of the mass media has primarily been conducted by academicians and journalists. Authors of social studies materials have apparently not been influenced by their writings. J. Herschel Parson's chapter "The Mass Media and Politics" is a fascinating study of various attempts by the mass media to attain consensus. Her chapter should be a valuable contribution to those who want to make the social studies curriculum more realistic.

The Domination of History at the Expense of the Social Sciences

The reader has only to think of his own secondary school courses in the social studies to realize that history has dominated the curriculum. Narrative history lends itself to the dramatic, the teacher's role as an actor naturally following. Yet, university historians are beginning to realize the value of the social sciences in general and the behavioral sciences in particular. It is now encumbent on those interested in social studies to find ways in which both the humanities and the social sciences may be given fair play. The editor's chapters on comparative approaches and the study of national character are designed to meet the previously mentioned challenge.

Conclusion

Social Studies as a curriculum area in secondary schools has a great distance to travel. Yet, recent ferment in the field gives us reason for optimism. Interest in the future of the social studies comes from many and diverse quarters. In the editor's opinion this diversity is healthy; it remains only for the secondary schools to tap those sources which will most appropriately meet their needs. This book is an effort to reach out on the frontiers of the social studies of tomorrow and provide those interested in social studies education with alternatives from which they can make their choices.

PART I

Social Studies and the
Culturally Disadvantaged

The Other America, by Michael Harrington, sparked the War on Poverty in the United States, and became not only the title of a book but an expression which is part of our everyday conversation. It naturally followed that the social studies would be expected to play an important role in reaching the victims of poverty in the United States. Of all the curriculum areas in the schools, the social studies area has been held primarily responsible for citizenship education. The term "social studies" is evidence of the social concern held by leaders in social studies education.

Yet, if one reviews the literature on the culturally disadvantaged, he finds a great deal written about the schools as a whole but relatively little on the social studies and the culturally disadvantaged. One reason for this neglect is that social studies educators and social studies teachers too often have not themselves worked with the culturally disadvantaged. As with Alexis de Tocqueville when he came to the United States in 1831-32, social studies educators and social studies teachers have too frequently spent too much time with the "nice" people. The more comfortable suburban environment—an environment which reinforces the teacher's own suburban experience— is chosen over the less secure but more demanding teaching in our urban slums. Both urban and suburban children suffer from the lack of contact between the two worlds.

The following chapter is written by a bright young journalist with the *Washington Post*. She has the advantage of being outside the educational establishment, thereby affording her a more objective, detached vantage point from which she can take a measure of our schools. As an education writer she has visited a variety of schools around the nation thus giving her a basis for comparison. She sees the schools as part of the larger society in which poverty exists. Her feeling for the culturally disadvantaged is evident in her excellent prose. Her conviction is contagious.

CHAPTER 1

Slum and Suburb:
the Neglected Reality

Susan Lynn Jacoby

Susan Lynn Jacoby is an education reporter for the Washington Post. *She received her B.A. from Michigan State University at the age of twenty and immediately began writing for the* Post. *She has spent several years covering the schools in Washington, D.C. and its suburbs. She has also been sent around the nation to observe urban and suburban social studies classes. Her article entitled "Education in Washington: National Monument to Failure" appeared in the* Saturday Review *in November of 1967.*

Traditional American education, it is generally conceded, has failed to meet the needs of deprived children who live in the nation's teeming urban ghettos. That failure is due in no small measure to the fact that the average school curriculum has virtually no relationship to the realities of life in a city slum; indeed, it has little relationship to the ferment that characterizes American life at all social levels. Peter Schrag, associate education editor of *Saturday Review,* has written of the Boston school system a perceptive study in which he indicts traditional curricula (and curriculum planners) for dealing "in cliches, in pieties, and in the tired liturgy of obsolete Americanisms which. . .by their nature—and by their intent, minimize the negative and unpleasant in American life—they exclude the possibilities of qualification and complexity, and the richness, the dynamic energy of controversy and ambiquity."[1]

This indictment is particularly damning when applied to the broad field of social studies, which by definition is the examination of human complexity, diversity, and controversy—both past and present. The neglected areas in the homogenized history, geography, and civics courses taught in most American elementary and secondary schools are legion. The condition of the Negro, the reality of poverty, the sharp class distinctions of modern society,

---

[1] Peter Schrag, *Villiage School Downtown* (Boston: Beacon Press, 1967), p. 90.

the increasing demands of dispossessed citizens for the kind of influence over their government that the wealthy have always held—these are only a few of the realities of American life that are daily ignored in many classrooms throughout the country.

It should be emphasized that these subjects are as neglected in the social studies curricula of white suburban schools as they are in the urban Negro ghetto schools. With the exception of a minority of courageous, perceptive teachers and an even smaller minority of innovative school systems, social studies courses seem dedicated to the proposition that to suggest the existence of anything other than the best of all possible worlds would be the equivalent of telling a dirty joke in a sex education class. This approach fails with slum children for the obvious reason that they have only to look out the classroom windows at the uncollected garbage, hopeless old men, and angry young men of the ghetto streets to realize that the shiny world the teacher talks about is at best a fiction, at worst a lie. Thus, the conventional social studies curriculum fails the urban child because it has no meaning in terms of his existence. The same curriculum fails the suburban child for the opposite reason: it does not acquaint him with anything outside of his own existence. The latter type of failure is graphically illustrated in *The Shortchanged Children of Suburbia,* a lengthy study conducted by a research team from Teachers College, Columbia University.

In one of the study's experiments, fifth-graders in a wealthy suburb of New York City were shown a picture of three poor white children. The youngsters in the picture were leaning against a fence, their hair stringy and dirty, their clothing ragged. Nearly all of the suburban students stoutly maintained that the children in the picture could not possibly be Americans. "You can tell by looking at them," said one fifth-grader. "No white children in our country would look like these three."[2] The teachers were astonished that their students could display such ignorance, even though they admitted that poverty was a subject rarely touched upon in the classroom. In another experiment in the same school system, children were shown a picture of a Negro boy playing with a white boy and asked which one they would choose for a friend. Nearly all picked the white boy. One second-grader explained he had chosen the white boy "because he didn't carry a knife."[3] (No knives were shown in the picture, of course.)

The Columbia study elicited an equally disturbing response from a Harlem teacher who asked his students to write a paper on their feeling about white people. Wrote one student: "White people says we Negroes need to take a bath. I saw a white man with nothing on in the window. White people want us to do all the dirty work. They don't want Negroes to have any fun." Said

[2]Alice Miel with Edwin Kiester, Jr., *The Shortchanged Children of Suburbia,* Pamphlet No. 8 (New York: Institute of Human Relations Press, 1967), p.23.

[3]*Ibid.,* p. 18.

another: "Whites have money and jewelry and diamonds and pearl bracelets and diamond earrings."[4] The responses of the Harlem students suggest that social studies educators, despite their white, middle-class orientation, conventional social studies curricula, and teaching methods, not only are failing to grapple with the realities of slum life but are failing to convey an accurate picture of middle-class America. The Harlem children have obviously never heard of thousands of white, middle-class Americans who declare bankruptcy each year (not to mention all of the white women who have never owned a pair of diamond earrings).

The Columbia study dealt with the entire school curriculum and its effect on students; however, many of its recommendations were concerned with social studies instruction as the logical vehicle for teaching elementary school children about human differences. The responsibility for communicating a sense of what Schrag calls "the richness, the dynamic energy of controversy and ambiguity" falls even more heavily on the high school social studies teacher as a result of departmentalization at the secondary level.

Before considering what might be done to improve social studies instruction, it is necessary to understand how and why traditional social studies curricula have neglected significant areas of human experience. Ignorance and timidity have always been the major causes of such neglect. Never were they more apparent than in the sometimes uninformed, sometimes unconscionable failure of social studies educators to teach their students about the history and culture of black Americans. Social studies educators—indeed the entire educational profession—are now attempting to make amends for that failure. The history of this transition has significant implications for every neglected area in the social studies.

In a lengthy article on traditional textbooks, one Negro magazine uses the not-so-facetious title of "Reading, 'Riting and Racism."[5] However, the sins of the textbook publishers—and the classroom teachers who used their materials—were generally those of omission rather than commission. There were simply no references to Negroes in textbooks published before the civil rights revolution of the early 1960's other than an occasional paragraph on the "happy darkies" who supposedly inhabited ante-bellum society in the South. No other ethnic group was as summarily ignored in the history books for so long a period of time. The Jewish and Italian and Chinese immigrants may have been called *kikes* and *wops* and *chinks* on the street, but in their texts they could read something about the contributions of their people to world history and culture (although the publishers tended to ignore the role of all minority groups in shaping the development of the United States).

In any case, the textbook publishers are now making a major effort to

[4]Stanley J. Albro, "Letters to the Editor," *The New York Times Magazine* (April 1967), p. 21.

[5]*Ebony*, Vol. XIII, No. 5 (March 1967), p. 130.

correct their past omissions in the area of Negro history. It does not speak well for social studies educators that the initial change in texts was spurred by demands from civil rights groups rather than from the educational profession. A secondary social studies supervisor in a highly regarded school system once remarked that the publishers develop textbooks to please every superintendent from Augusta, Me., to Augusta, Ga. He might also have noted that educators in Maine are just as responsible for the problem as the publishers if they accept the Georgia versions without quibbling. Publishers respond with surprising speed to new demands from school systems; if the educators had asked for a thorough treatment of Negro history in textbooks, the change would undoubtedly have come earlier. During the past two years, several state legislatures have passed laws requiring the teaching of Negro history. This legislation has been supported by organizations of professional educators, including social studies teachers, but has not been initiated by them. In fairness, it must be noted that the adoption of "multi-ethnic" textbooks in large cities has been given a strong push by militant teacher unions demanding a greater voice in curriculum planning. In Detroit, a contract between the public school system and its teachers spells out the expansion of Negro history instruction as one of the terms of the agreement.

There is some evidence indicating that Negro history may be in danger of the same type of homogenization that has turned the rest of American history into a bland gruel for elementary and secondary school consumption. Every child with a textbook published after 1965 is likely to learn that Crispus Attucks, a Negro, was the first soldier to die in the Revolutionary War and that a Negro doctor named Charles Drew was the developer of blood plasma. All textbooks published after 1967 will undoubtedly record that Thurgood Marshall was the first Negro appointed to the Supreme Court. But will the same textbooks record the words of Stokely Carmichael in the steaming summer ghettos? Will the riots of Harlem and Watts receive more careful attention than uprisings of workers in the nineteenth century or earlier racial disturbances in the twentieth century? Will the agony of the Reverend Martin Luther King, Jr. over Vietnam be explored, or will the textbooks simply record that he won the Nobel Peace Prize? In viewing the past record of textbook publishers and social studies educators, it would be foolish to conclude that a new era of sophistication is in the offing simply because a few black faces have been accorded their rightful places in the history books.

In many cases, social studies educators smooth over reality with flag-waving clichés because they have too little confidence in the ability of their students to perceive complexity. Subjects such as the structure of the Negro family are often assumed to be beyond the comprehension of secondary students—not to mention elementary school children. On the basis of my experience as an observer in elementary and secondary schools, I regard this as a false assumption. I have watched a fourth grade teacher in a Washington,

D.C., slum school conduct a superb discussion of the effects of slavery on the Negro family. The children—all of them classified as "slow learners"—were quite capable of understanding how and why the families of slaves were broken up in the ante-bellum South. As they advance in school, these youngsters will be just as capable of comprehending the relationship between what happened to slaves in the eighteenth and nineteenth centuries and the state of many fatherless Negro families in urban ghettos today. However, the children may not have the good fortune to encounter another teacher with enough sensitivity and courage to bring such a delicate subject into the classroom.

In general, textbook publishers, classroom teachers, and administrators share the same assumptions about the unsuitability of "unpleasant" subjects for young students. One representative of a major publishing company had this to say when I questioned him about the omission of a realistic discussion of slavery in his company's widely used fifth grade American history text: "We think the function of a student's first history text is to build patriotism, not to tell all of the nasty facts of our history. This is better for an older child." The publisher's attitude is based on two highly debatable assumptions—that the primary function of an American history course is to build patriotism and that a child is likely to be less patriotic if he learns anything about the less glorious chapters of the nation's development. Interestingly enough, the popular fifth grade history book with only a cursory treatment of slavery is used in Washington, D.C., and several other large cities for "slow readers" in eighth- and ninth-grade classes. One can only imagine the boredom with which a tough fourteen year old from a city ghetto—who is usually older in experience than a middle-class college student—greets a history book that would not challenge a bright ten year old.

The combination of ignorance and timidity that has hampered inquiring, objective social studies education is apparent in both city and suburb. The principal of Washington's all-Negro Hine Junior High School objected strongly last winter when an eight-grader wrote a composition—later published in the city's newspapers—about how it feels to be a Negro when white people make fun of you. "You walk down the street to hear a white person call you names," wrote the student. "We will rise against our time to prove to people that we are dying to show that we are human beings, and not just some people from another world." Principal John C. Hoffman said, "I don't approve of that sort of thing. It can only cause bad feelings."[6] In neighboring Montgomery County, Md., which has the highest per capita income of any suburban community in the country, a former school board president attacked the idea of exchange programs with city schools. "I don't think there are great strengths to be recognized by mingling races or people from different economic groups in an artificial situation," he said. "For one thing, I think an

[6]*The Washington Post*, March 4, 1967, p. B-1.

exchange program between the District of Columbia and Montgomery County, Md., would make the poorer children discontented with what they have. You know—'the grass is always greener.' And I think the children in the suburbs are already aware that others are less fortunate. They get this when they give to collections for the needy at church and school, and through community services."[7] These types of attitudes are inevitably reflected in school curricula. However, a minority of bold school systems and teachers are demonstrating that this need not be so—that it is possible to devise a social studies curriculum related to the realities of life in both the urban and suburban sectors of the nation's sprawling metropolises.

Two high schools, one in Washington, D.C., and the other in Montgomery County, Md., have produced an outstanding, widely publicized example of how a carefully developed social studies curriculum can come to grips with problems such as race and poverty. Cardozo High School, with a 100 percent Negro enrollment, is located in the heart of an impoverished city ghetto and Walt Whitman High School is located in Montgomery's richest census tract. Women from the Cardozo area take the bus out of the city every day to work as maids in the sprawling $75,000 homes that surround Walt Whitman. The idea for an exchange program between the two schools originated in an American history class at Walt Whitman, where a young teacher named Michaela Carberry was trying to tell her students something about the differences between education in an affluent suburb and in a city slum. When a student suggested that it might be useful for the class to visit an inner city school to view the differences firsthand, Miss Carberry pointed out that it would be difficult to learn very much through a "one-shot" visit. She discussed the problem with the head of her social studies department, who agreed that the social studies curriculum was a logical vehicle for piercing the economic, cultural, and racial isolation of the students at Walt Whitman. Miss Carberry's department head contacted the director of an unusual project at Cardozo which attempts to give college graduates with bachelor's degrees on-the-job training to enable them to meet the special needs of disadvantaged students. The idea was turned over to Bill Plitt, a former Peace Corps volunteer who was a teaching intern in the Cardozo project.

Both teachers wanted their classes to actually study American history together, and they held several meetings with committees of their students to plan a curriculum. The teachers suggested that the classes study a unit on civil rights as a joint venture, but the students felt they would learn more by beginning with slavery. The curriculum was ultimately worked out to include slavery, reconstruction, urbanization, and civil rights. The two classes studied the same material and met together once a week, alternating between Cardozo and Walt Whitman. Activities at the joint meetings were highly unorthodox and highly interesting to the students. At one session, a play on slavery was

[7]*The Washington Post*, January 10, 1966, p. C-1.

presented in which the white students from Walt Whitman took the parts of slaves and the Negro students from Cardozo took the parts of masters which led to a lively, open discussion about why the students had felt slightly uncomfortable in the reversed roles a hundred years after emancipation. Most of the students responded enthusiastically, although a few admitted they were not used to such frank talk and never would have thought it possible in an interracial class. The class eventually led to an exchange program in which the students lived at each other's houses and attended classes at each other's schools for a week. Parents were almost as enthusiastic about the program as their teenage sons and daughters. "My husband and I are from the South," said one Negro mother, "and we honestly aren't used to any kind of contact between white and colored. We know our children will live in a different kind of world and it seems right that the schools should prepare them." Commented a white father: "We're having all this fuss over open occupancy laws in the county. I'm convinced that half of the people who are doing all the shouting have never known a Negro as a friend. The schools should be making every effort through their curriculum to provide these kinds of experiences for kids."

The students' reactions are even more instructive. The crucial advantage of the program seems to have been that the students learned more about American history at the same time they were learning more about each other. "I never could have learned as much about urban problems sitting in the classroom as I did through this program," said one suburban boy. "When I told the kids I was going down to Cardozo to spend a week, I got all the usual cracks about how all the Negro kids learn is street fighting in gym class. I've managed to educate a lot of my friends since I got back."

The Cardozo-Whitman program lasted for about six months of the 1966-67 school year and will be expanded next year to include more students. The program was neither expensive nor elaborate; its main ingredients were imagination and determination on the part of two teachers. In isolated instances around the country, other schools are embarking on equally noteworthy projects designed to bring the social studies curriculum to grips with the realities of urban life. At New Trier High School in Evanston, Ill., school officials felt they were not doing enough to broaden the experience of their affluent students despite New Trier's national reputation for academic excellence. Next year, they plan to use the city of Chicago as a laboratory for social studies classes. New Trier students will work in the city's schools, settlement houses, and playgrounds for credit in various high school courses. Rochester, N.Y., is involved in a far-reaching experiment that goes beyond social studies. A new school located in the central city will draw half of its enrollment from nearby suburbs and half from Rochester's ghetto schools. With small classes, outstanding teachers, and an enriched curriculum in every subject—particularly social studies, science, and English—the school already has a waiting list of applicants from the suburbs and the city. The Rochester experiment will be expensive, and a project of this kind obviously cannot be carried on by social studies educators alone. But programs such as those at Cardozo-Whitman and New Trier are within the reach of every imaginative social studies teacher and administrator; their outstanding characteristic is that they make use of the materials at hand. The development of a more meaningful social studies curriculum can only be achieved if teachers do make better use of the materials at hand to bring not only race and poverty but countless other meaningful aspects of modern civilization into the classroom. How many teachers, for example, would have the imagination to impress their students with a lesson on the Depression by having them present a play on how it feels to be evicted by a landlord? Poverty-stricken students in city ghettos live in their own personal depression; by using experiences from their lives, a social studies teacher can reach them when conventional history books fail. The same holds true for suburban schools. How many high school sociology teachers would suggest that their students study their own teenage class structure as a means of furthering their understanding of the communities in which they live? Social studies educators have too often been guilty of what the newspaper profession calls "Afghanistanism"—an overwillingness to comment on events in far corners of the globe and a noticeable reluctance to come to grips with problems at home. In an outstanding suburban school system in the East, a complete revamping of the social studies curriculum was precipitated by a caustic report outlining the irrelevence of social studies instruction at the elementary level. The report noted that one elementary school social studies unit was designed to instruct children in "Organizing an International Travel Bureau."[8] (The same curriculum did make some attempt to discuss nearby problems. One of the liveliest units: "Attracting Birds to Our School Grounds.")[9]

Incidents that may foster timidity in social studies teachers can occur in any community; some examples have been enumerated here. It is my opinion that the social studies educator—indeed, the entire educational profession— must lead public opinion rather than follow it in frightened, hangdog fashion. The specter of angry parents banging on the principal's door looms too large. Teachers and administrators are too often cowed by a vocal minority; in such cases, they fail to make the effort needed to "sell" imaginative programs to the majority of parents. Projects such as the Cardozo-Whitman exchange demonstrate that social studies courses can serve an educational function for the entire community and not merely for students enrolled in school. There is no magic formula for conquering timidity when it is deeply ingrained in teachers and administrators. Overcoming teacher ignorance, however, is a

[8]*The Washington Post,* April 15, 1961, p. 31.
[9]*Ibid.*

process that can be fostered by school systems through a series of logical steps.

One of the greatest hindrances to the development of meaningful social studies education is the dichotomy between secondary school teachers and college professors in the social sciences. In too many cases, outstanding high school social studies teachers are only marking time until they can earn their doctorates and move on to the college level. Having left the field to football coaches who for some mysterious reason are often pressed into service as civics and history teachers, they sneer at the poor preparation and naiveté of the students who come to them as freshman. This dichotomy is the result of an educational structure that was designed for a largely rural society. Local school boards, jealous of their perogatives, are often totally indifferent to the idea of cooperation with nearby colleges. In the past, most colleges have been just as indifferent. However, educational planners are beginning to recognize that colleges and universities can no longer operate independently of public elementary and secondary schools as they did in the days when only a tiny minority of students continued their education beyond the twelfth grade. There are many outstanding examples of this recognition, but most of them are not in the field of social studies. In Ft. Lauderdale, Fla., the Nova Schools are developing an elementary and secondary curriculum in oceanography and the physical sciences. Students can continue in the same curriculum at a nearby public junior college and will eventually be able to do advanced work at Nova University, a private graduate school. Social studies educators have not embarked on this type of planning for a variety of reasons—most of them connected with the way elementary and secondary teachers are trained in schools of education.

Most high school social studies teachers do not know enough about their subject matter. I sat in one American history class this year in which a teacher was astonished when one of her students mentioned that the Mexican War was a topic of dissent in the nineteenth century just as the Vietnam war is today. This type of ignorance can be laid directly at the door of teacher training that places more emphasis on how to teach then on whether the teacher knows anything about his (or her) academic discipline. Social studies teachers at the high school level tend to ignore the fact that the subjects they teach *are,* in fact, academic disciplines. Consequently, the social studies teacher with a scholarly bent feels cut off from the intellectual life of his profession if he remains in a high school. All of this is not to say that a high school American history teacher should know as much about his subject as a college professor dealing with graduate students. It is to say, however, that his major field of study in college should have been history and not physical education. To improve elementary and secondary school social studies instruction, teachers must be oriented more toward the inductive approach that characterizes academic disciplines at the university level. One recent study of social studies curricula throughout the United States puts it succinctly: "Some years ago the Educational Policies Commission published a statement to the effect that the central purpose of American education is the development of rational thinking. Our task is to provide the means of accomplishing this goal. . .We need and are getting more and better teacher training; we need and are getting better curriculum materials. However, we need and are *not* getting better curriculum materials. However, we need and are not getting sufficient commitment on the part of teachers to inquiry-oriented teaching."[10] That commitment, backed up with knowledge and courage, is the only way to bring the social studies curriculum to grips with the realities of urban life. In essence, the social studies teacher must say to the child in a slum school: "This is your world. I understand it." To the suburban child, he must say: "Your world is not the only world."

Annotated Bibliography

Goldstein, Bernard, *Low Income Youth in Urban Areas.* Holt, Rinehart and Winston, Inc., New York, 1967. The most definitive critical review of the literature dealing with culturally disadvantaged youth. Fully annotated and most helpful source for those interested in getting to the literature on the culturally disadvantaged.

Hickerson, Nathaniel, *Education for Alienation.* Prentice-Hall, Inc., Englewood Cliffs, N.J., 1966. The author, who is the Director of Education for Western United States Anti-Defamation League, attempts to show how our public schools, as mirrors of our society, have played an important role in creating the conditions which have led to the waste of talent and ability and the subsequent loss of dignity and self-worth. Part Four titled "Curriculum for the Economically Deprived" is outstanding.

Kerber, August, and Bommarito, Barbara (eds.), *The Schools and the Urban Crisis.* Holt, Rinehart and Winston, Inc., New York, 1965. The basis for this compilation of readings is the editors' belief that the greatest challenge facing public education today is that of preparing students adequately for adult life in a complex and changing urban society.

Landes, Ruth, *Culture in American Education: Anthropological Approaches to Minority and Dominant Groups in the Schools.* John Wiley & Sons, New York, 1965. This book describes the Anthropology and Education program

---

[10]William D. Rader, "The Intermediate Grades," in C. Benjamin Cox and Byron G. Massialas, eds., *Social Studies in the United States: A Critical Appraisal* (New York: Harcourt, Brace & World, Inc., 1967), p. 49.

conducted at the Claremont Graduate School from 1959-61. The main minority groups dealt with consisted of Negroes and Mexican-Americans.

Nordstrom, Carl, Friedenberg, Edgar Z., and Gold, Hilary A., *Society's Children.* Random House, Inc., New York, 1967. A sociological and philosophical analysis which attempts to measure the malevolent influence of ressentiment on school environments. Deals with secondary schools.

Passow, A. Harry, Goldbert, Miriam, and Tannenbaum, Abraham J. (eds.), *Education of the Disadvantaged.* Holt, Rinehart and Winston, Inc., New York, 1967. Deals with the nature and setting of the educational problem, disadvantaged minority groups, socio-psychological factors affecting school achievement, education for the disadvantaged, and teachers for the disadvantaged. An excellent compilation of readings.

Sexton, Patricia Cayo, *Education and Income.* The Viking Press, Inc., New York, 1961. A study of the inequalities of opportunity in our public schools. The relationship between social class and education is explored. Focus is on the big city schools. An excellent volume.

Strom, Robert D., *Teaching in the Slum School.* Charles E. Merrill Books, Inc., Columbus, Ohio, 1965. A discussion of urban slums, inner-city schools, the preparation and recruitment of teachers, school staffs, classroom instruction, and prospects for change. Deals with the larger problem of social setting as well as the schools themselves.

Webster, Staten W. (ed.), *Educating the Disadvantaged Learner.* Chandler Publishing Company, San Francisco, 1966. This volume of readings is divided into two sections. Articles dealing with school, teacher, and community problems relating to the disadvantaged learner are found in the first section dealing with "Problems in the Education of the Disadvantaged." The second section deals with "The Process of Educating the Disadvantaged Learner."

——, *Knowing the Disadvantaged.* Chandler Publishing Company, San Francisco, 1966. The editor has organized a series of readings according to the sociocultural approach to increased understanding of the disadvantaged learner. Outstanding chapters are written by Michael Harrington, Robert J. Havighurst, Frank Riessman, and George D. and Louise S. Spindler.

——, *Understanding the Educational Problems of the Disadvantaged Learner.* Chandler Publishing Company, San Francisco, 1966. Readings discuss the problems of disadvantaged learners in the areas of language, social studies, and mathematics.

PART II

Religion, Philosophy, and the Social Studies

The following section deals with moral values and the social studies. This discussion is very important in the light of the social studies teacher's concern with the "good citizenship" − inquiry confrontation. That is, many define good citizenship in such a way that inquiry is stifled; at the same time there is concern on the part of others that inquiry at the expense of socialization will lead to what Emile Durkheim called "anomic normlessness," an extreme form of alienation which is most difficult for the citizen to cope with in an industrial age.

Religions provide us with the most dramatic example of moral beliefs, and therefore are closely related to moral education in the schools. This relationship is explored in Chapter 2 by Robert S. Michaelsen. His chapter is a very clear analysis of a most complicated subject.

Philosophy as an academic discipline has not traditionally been a part of the secondary social studies curriculum. Fraught with controversy, this discipline is somewhat of an enigma to the social studies teacher. Yet, there is general agreement that the social studies teacher may learn a great deal from the study of philosophy. Chapter 3, by W. Eugene Hedley, discusses the part that philosophy as a formal discipline may play in the social studies of the future.

Both Professors Michaelsen and Hedley are fully cognizant of the dual expectations for the social studies functions: the analytical, and the socializing.

CHAPTER 2

The Public Schools and "America's Two Religions"*

Robert S. Michaelsen[1]

Robert S. Michaelsen is Chairman of the Department of Religious Studies at the University of California, Santa Barbara. He is author of The Study of Religion in American Universities *and is presently completing a book on religion and the public schools in the United States.*

"Our schools, in bringing together those of different nationalities, traditions and creeds, in assimilating them together upon the basis of what is common and public in endeavor and achievement, are performing an infinitely significant religious work."[2]

"The work of public education is with us . . ., to a large degree, a piece of religious work."[3]

". . . .The public schools in the United States took over one of the basic responsibilities that traditionally was always assumed by an established church. In this sense the public-school system of the United States *is* its established church."[4]

---

*Reprinted from A Journal of Church and State, VIII (Autumn 1966), pp. 380-400. Used by permission.

[1] I am indebted to my former colleague, Professor Sidney E. Mead, for the phraseology and the concept of "America's Two Religions" and for much of the basic thesis of this chapter. See especially his "The Post-Protestant Concept and America's Two Religions," *Religion in Life,* XXXIII (Spring 1964), pp. 191-204; and *The Lively Experiment* (New York: Harper & Row, Publishers, 1963), pp. 66ff and 135ff.

[2] John Dewey, "Religion and Our Schools," *The Hibbert Journal,* VI (July 1908), 796-809, reprinted in *Characters and Events,* II (New York: H. Holt and Co., 1929), pp. 504-516.

[3] Ellwood P. Cubberley, *Changing Conceptions of Education* (New York: Houghton Mifflin Company, 1909), p. 68.

[4] Mead, *The Lively Experiment, op. cit.,* p. 68.

Introduction

Few issues have stimulated the expenditure of more intellectual and emotional energy among the American people than the question of the relationship between religion and public education. Within the last two decades the United States Supreme Court alone has deliberated and decided at least a half dozen cases bearing directly on this question. And these cases have stimulated enough comment, criticism, speculation, and prediction to constitute a small library. The testimony on the so-called Becker prayer amendment, given before the House Judiciary Committee in 1963, fills three volumes, each as lengthy, although perhaps not as edifying, as the Holy Bible. More recently, Senator Everett McKinley Dirksen, after filibustering against efforts to achieve open housing in a civil rights measure, has devoted himself with appropriate moral and religious zeal to the passage of his own prayer amendment. A bibliography on "The School Question" lists about 2,000 titles for the twenty-year period from 1940 to 1960.[5] When James Bryant Conant, who was President of Harvard at the time, delivered a brief address on "Unity and Diversity in Secondary Education" to a session of the American Association of School Administrators in April of 1952, his shot, while it may not have been heard around the world like the one fired at near-by Lexington 173 years earlier, did evoke a noisy and voluminous response.

This issue is not new, nor has it become the subject of public discussion only in our generation. For example, a review of popular, religious, and scholarly journals in the late nineteenth century would turn up more relevant articles; the question was very much a public political issue during the presidential terms of Grant and Hayes; the controversies over religion and public education in such states as Massachusetts and New York in the years before the Civil War have been thesis subjects of enough M.A.'s and Ph.D.'s to staff the faculty of a liberal arts college; and that the relevant writings of Thomas Jefferson alone among the founding fathers are sizable and meaty enough not only to keep the ordinary reader occupied for some months, but have also produced an enormous amount of commentary from his day down to the present.

What excuse is there, then, for adding to this great volume of discussion? Aside from the fact that this is just the sort of issue which should be discussed by the American people, it is the position of this chapter that (1) historical perspective can be helpful in understanding and assessing the present situation; and (2) the issue can be further illumined by examining it in a broader theoretical or theological context than has been customary. The achievement of these two points requires compressing two centuries of history into a brief space

---

[5] *The School Question: A Bibliography on Church-State Relationships in American Education, 1940-1960,* compiled by Edmond G. Drouin (Washington, D.C.: The Catholic University of America Press, 1963).

and drawing, or overdrawing, some sharp pictures of a commonly overlooked aspect of our situation.

The basic thesis of this essay requires a distinction between what I shall call "religion A" – organized, institutionalized religion, the religion of the denominations, whether Jewish, Catholic, or Protestant (Methodist, Lutheran, Baptist, or Mormon) – on the one hand, and "religion B" – the common faith, the democratic proposition – on the other. Furthermore, I shall argue that the public school has been accepted in America as the primary institution for the achievement and inculcation of the latter and has had, from its beginnings down to the present, an ambivalent relationship to the former.

The Corpus Christianum and the Corpus Americanum

What is necessary to the achievement and functioning of a commonwealth, a nation? All or nearly all of the following elements: a system of effective government, a viable economy, a common language, a common history, common ideals, hopes, assumptions–a common faith, if you will–and institutions for effectively inculcating these common elements among citizens and the youth who are to become citizens. For more than a thousand years Christianity furnished much of the necessary substrata in the West–the common faith–and the Church was the most effective instrument for passing the common elements on from generation to generation. This was the age of the *Corpus Christianum,* the Christian society or civilization. Although this society was in process of rapid change and even break-up in the seventeenth century, many of the American colonists brought both the idea and the practice with them. Thus the Puritans and the Anglicans sought to set up Christian commonwealths in which church and state were closely linked and education was under Christian control. But by this time, and even by the sixteenth century, the West was facing the brute fact of religious pluralism.[6] And the founding fathers of the American republic were faced with the necessity of dealing with this religious pluralism, which had become even more evident by the late eighteenth century. At the same time, they had to arrive at and agree upon a common faith in constituting the new commonwealth and to devise methods for inculcating that faith.

The fact of religious pluralism was dealt with through constitutional provisions prohibiting religious tests for federal office holders and providing that "Congress shall make no law respecting an establishment of religion or

[6]For example, note the formula, *cuius regio, eius religio,* which was followed in most American colonies, and which was a device for dealing on the one hand with the realities of pluralism within Christianity, and on the other hand, for preserving something of the pattern and ideal of the *Corpus Christianum.*

prohibiting the free exercise thereof."[7] No church was to be the established church of the federal government. "Religion A" was to have no formal 'relationship to the machinery of the federal government.

What, then, would be the common faith, the glue to hold the new society together, the common memories and aspirations that would give the people a sense of identity? This faith was most succinctly stated in the Declaration of Independence and most clearly elaborated in the writings of the founding fathers—especially those of Franklin, Paine, Jefferson, and Madison.

> We hold these truths to be self-evident, that all men are created equal, that they are endowed by their Creator with certain unalienable rights, that among these are life, liberty, and the pursuit of happiness. That to secure these rights, governments are instituted among men . . . .

This statement from the Declaration of Independence embodies the fundamental philosophy underlying the democratic experiment, the confession of faith of the founding fathers and the American people.[8] Certainly there are elements of Christianity or of the Judeo-Christian tradition in this faith. But there are also elements which differ from historical Christianity; elements from eighteenth century rationalistic deism; elements which the fathers regarded as being common to all religions, the best in all religions, and the only aspect of any religion necessary to civic order and public well-being. I call this democratic faith "religion B." It can be called a religion because it involves basic assumptions about man, society, and the universe; and because it has performed a religious function in the life of the American people.

Given the common faith, what was to be the instrumentality for inculcating it? The churches? Perhaps, but only to a limited extent, not because the churches disagreed with the democratic proposition but because they disagreed among themselves. Nor could the task be assigned to schools solely under the control of the churches, for this would produce disagreement and disunity over questions that mattered most. What was needed, and Jefferson saw this clearly from the beginning, was a system of public or common education, open to all, financed by taxation, and under the direction of no particular or sectarian group; a system from which "religion A" would be excluded because of its sectarian (and, for Jefferson, private) nature, and "religion B" would be instilled because of its unifying nature. Thus the public school would become the

---

[7]See Article VI of the Constitution. The quotation is the first phrase of the first amendment to the Constitution.

[8]"America is the only nation in the world founded on a creed," observed G. K. Chesterton. So "far as its primary ideal is concerned," America's "exclusiveness is religious. . . . " The theory of equality is basic to this creed, "the pure classic conception that no man must aspire to be anything more than a citizen, and that no man shall endure to be anything less." "What Is America?" in Raymond T. Bond, ed. *The Man Who Was Chesterton* (New York: Dodd, Mead & Company, 1937), pp. 188ff.

primary instrumentality for Americanization, for democratization, and for the achievement of unity in the common faith. It is in this sense that we can refer to the public school as being America's established church.[9]

The "Establishment" of the Public School

The story of the development of popular education in the United States is one of increasing movement away from sectarian control and sectarian teaching (increasing "secularization"), on the one hand, and increasing acknowledgement of the public school as the primary institution of democratization and Americanization, on the other. By 1876, one century after the affirmations of the Declaration of Independence, the majority of the American people had accepted the principle and desirability of a universal free public school system, free from sectarian control and teaching, and as essential to the life of the democratic republic. States admitted to the Union after that year were required by Congress to provide, "by ordinance irrevocable without the consent of the United States and the people of said States . . . for the establishment and maintenance of systems of public schools, which shall be open to all the children of said States and free from sectarian control . . . ."[10] Most of the older states had already adopted some such provision, either constitutional or statutory, by 1876.

Measures of the strength of sentiment for the public school in the late nineteenth century can be found in the writings of public educators, politicians, and Protestant clergymen, and in the prevailing attitude toward those (chiefly Roman Catholics) who did not share this sentiment. "Democracy necessitates the public school," affirmed the Protestant preacher, Josiah Strong, in his widely read book, *Our Country*.[11] "The public school is and ever will be an American institution . .," asserted the church historian, Philip Schaff, in his discussion of church and state. It is essential to the well-being of the "democratic republic."[12] "The public school system of the several states is the bulwark of the American Republic . . .," declared the Republican National Platform of 1876 in a plank

[9]A significant measure of the importance Jefferson attached to public education is to be found in the fact that he wished to extend the scope of government only in the single direction of popular education.

[10]As quoted by Associate Justice Frankfurter in *McCollum* v. *Board of Education,* 330 U.S. 203, 220 n. 9.

[11]Josiah Strong, *Our Country,* rev. ed., Jurgen Herbst, ed. (Cambridge, Mass.: Harvard University Press, 1963), p. 89. First published in 1886, over 175,000 copies had sold by 1916, and individual chapters had been reprinted in newspapers and magazines and published separately in pamphlet form.

[12]*Church and State in the United States* (New York: G. P. Putnam's Sons, 1888), p. 74.

which called for an amendment to the U.S. Constitution "forbidding the application of any public funds or property for the benefit of any schools . . . under sectarian control."[13] "Under our form of government," wrote President Grant in his message to Congress in 1875, "the education of the masses becomes the first necessity for the preservation of our institutions."[14] Much of this sort of discussion among politicians was directed against a defeated South and a weakened Democratic Party, and much of the discussion among religious leaders was directed against Roman Catholicism. Strong labeled the Catholic Church as "un-American" because it did not support the public school. And while no Catholic authority ever for one moment agreed to that charge, Cardinal Gibbons did explain to Pope Leo XIII, in defending Archbishop Ireland's relatively liberal position on religion and public education, that the Catholic position on parochial schools was one of the chief causes of anti-Catholicism in America.[15]

E Pluribus Unum

But why was the public school so essential to the public welfare? Because democracy required an educated public? True. But equally as important, because democracy required unity among the people. The public school was the institution par excellence for achieving the goal expressed in the motto on the great seal: *E Pluribus Unum*, from many, one. It was this function that John Dewey had in mind when in 1908 he wrote the statement quoted at the beginning of this paper. It was this that President Grant had in mind when he urged a constitutional amendment "making it the duty of the several States to establish and forever maintain free public schools adequate to the education of all children . . ., irrespective of sex, color, birthplace, or religious. . . ."[16] It was this that Strong was conscious of when he stressed that democracy necessitated the public school in America, "for in the United States the common school has a function which is peculiar, viz., to Americanize the children of immigrants."[17] And it was probably the same sort of motivation which prompted over 100,000 citizens of Oregon to take the apparently logical step in the early 1920's of requiring all children through the age of sixteen to attend the *public* school.[18]

[13]Lamar T. Beman, *Religious Teaching in the Public Schools* (New York: H. W. Wilson Co., 1927), pp. 74ff.

[14]*Documents of American Catholic History*, John Tracy Ellis, ed., (Milwaukee, Wisc.: The Bruce Publishing Co., 1962), p. 392.

[15]*Ibid.*, p. 469.

[16]*Ibid.*, p.393.

[17]Strong, *op. cit.*, p. 89.

[18]This law was declared unconstitutional by the U.S. Supreme Court in 1924 before it actually became effective in Oregon. *Pierce* v. *Society of Sisters*, 268 U.S. 510. For fuller detail see *Oregon School Cases, Complete Record* (Baltimore, Md.: The Belvedere Press, 1925).

E Pluribus Unum, and the role of the public school in achieving it, took on special significance and became crucially important in the century or more in which America absorbed millions of immigrants. The preeminent task was one of getting these diverse peoples to live together, speak the same language, and come to share common ideals. From this experience there emerged the figure of the "melting pot" to describe the American ideal.

What relevance does the "melting pot" ideal have today, now that the millions of immigrants have been almost completely absorbed? Actually, some elements would not melt, even at boiling point. You could teach a German to speak English, and make an American out of a Swede or a Pole. But it was much more difficult to make a Protestant out of a Catholic or Jew and physically impossible to make a white man out of a Negro. In reality, as Will Herberg points out, the "melting pot" was actually a "transmuting pot" by which diverse elements were made to conform to or approximate the American ideal—which until relatively recently at least, was the WASP ideal, that is, White, Anglo-Saxon, Protestant.[19] Thus the ideal had to be broadened or made to accord more with the original affirmation: "that all men are created equal." And we are still struggling valiantly in the schools and elsewhere with "democracy's unfinished business" in the area of race.

What about religion? The *Unum* has never implied Protestant only, in a narrow sense; nevertheless, it is true that non-Protestants, and especially Jews and Catholics, have not always been accorded their full rights as Americans. And we continue to seek the nature and fullness of the meaning of the motto, to achieve unity in or from our diversity. The public school is still regarded by many as the primary agency for realizing this goal. While it is true that the "task of assimilating many strains of migrations has been accomplished," President Conant observed in 1952, still " the job of nourishing the spirit of democratic unity continues. This is the task of the public school, and especially the public high school," Conant maintained, "and movement in the direction of a dual system of public and private schools is a threat to American unity and thus a threat to the democratic way of life."[20] For Conant, then, as for Dewey and many others, religious differences are especially regrettable and problematic when they separate young Americans into differing groups, whether within the public school itself or in public schools and parochial schools. The ideal situation continues to be, in their minds, one in which all or nearly all American youth attend the *common* school where they achieve unity in diversity. Thus the public school continues to be the established church.[21]

John Dewey himself was most articulate in seeing the role of the public

---

[19]*Protestant, Catholic, Jew,* rev. ed. (Garden City, N.Y.: Doubleday & Company, Inc. 1960).

[20]*Education and Liberty: The Role of the Schools in A Modern Democracy* (Cambridge, Mass.: Harvard University Press, 1953), p. 62 and Chapter III.

[21]It "is our strong belief that all the youth of all the people should be educated together

school as being *religious* because of its crucial importance in Americanizing and democratizing the youth. Here they achieve a sense of self-identity and group consciousness as Americans and as human beings. And this is "an infinitely significant religious work" because the public schools "are promoting the social unity out of which in the end genuine religious unity must grow." Under the proper conditions, Dewey observed, "schools are more religious in substance and in promise without any of the conventional badges and machinery of religious instruction than they could be in cultivating these forms at the expense of a state-consciousness."[22] In Dewey, then, and in likeminded individuals, we have a powerful twentieth century expression of the idea of the public school as America's "established church." Theirs is a position which raises a host of questions, and as such, their position has elicited equally powerful reactions in opposition. But this much is to be said for this position: It is consistent; it forces us to think seriously about the nature of the democratic faith, the democratic proposition, and the role of the schools in achieving and inculcating the democratic "way of life."

Religion A and Religion B in the Public School

One of the fundamental questions which the position of Dewey and others raises is what will be taught in the public school with regard to both religion A and religion B. Their answer is that religion A must be excluded from the public school precisely because it is divisive. Dewey distinguished between "religion" (i.e., religion A) and the "religious" (i.e., religion B), and relegated the former to the private realm and to the churches while stressing the importance of the latter for the public well-being.[23]

---

in the common public school . . .," affirmed the authors of the Seventh Yearbook of The John Dewey Society. They acknowledged the "legal right" of "any local group" to organize a private school, but they saw such efforts as inherent threats "to the democratic process" if they became more than local, that is, if they came to involve any substantial number of American youth. *The Public Schools and Spiritual Values,* John S. Brubacher, ed. (New York: Harper & Row, Publishers, 1944), p. 6. Cf. Professor Philip Kurland's conclusions with regard to parochial schools: "My own reading of the Supreme Court cases leads me to the conclusion that aid to parochial schools is not unconstitutional, so long as it takes a nondiscriminatory form. I am at least equally convinced that the segregation of school children by religion is an unmitigated evil." *Religion and The Law* (Chicago: Aldine Publishing Co., 1962), p. 9.

[22]"Religion and Our Schools," *op. cit.,* p. 514. While Dewey penned these words in 1908 his view of the "religious" role of the public school did not change appreciably during the remainder of his life. See his "Education as a Religion," *The New Republic,* XXXII, (September 1922), pp. 64-65, reprinted in John S. Brubacher, ed., *Eclectric Philosophy of Education,* 2d ed. (Englewood Cliffs, N.J.: Prentice-Hall, Inc., 1962), pp. 537-538; and *A Common Faith* (New Haven, Conn.: Yale University Press, 1934).

[23]This thesis is most fully developed in *A Common Faith, op. cit.*

It is well known that Dewey stressed "learning by doing." Thus religion B, the common faith, is best acquired when all the youth can live, work, study, learn, and play together—when they engage in common activities. But, when pushed to be explicit about *what* is taught of a religious nature as well as *how* it is taught, Dewey and others of similar mind have pointed to the *values* of democracy and of a kind of basic humanism. Dewey labeled these values "religious." Others have been somewhat less direct and have called them "spiritual."[24] The Educational Policies Commission of the National Education Association and the American Association of School Administrators used and popularized the designation "Moral and Spiritual Values."[25] These are the values held in common by the American people and these values are achieved, learned, and passed on in the public school. But the questions of the relationship of these values to religion, i.e., to religion A, and of the school's role with regard to religion A, remain as bothersome questions with which the American people continue to wrestle.

It is helpful at this juncture, then, to have a look at what the public schools have taught with regard to religion, both A and B, and what formulators of policies related to public school practice and curriculum have maintained in this respect.

"Sectarianism" and The Common Faith

It is clear that the story of the development of the public school system in the United States can be told in part in terms of increasing movement away from sectarian control and sectarian teaching. But what is "sectarian?" For Jefferson, anything other than the essentials held in common by all religions was sectarian. In most of the legislative acts and in the minds of most leading educators of the nineteenth century, "sectarian" meant the particular or distinctive teachings of any organized religious group, of any "sect." It was obvious, then, that any school established and operated by a "sect" was under sectarian control if not sectarian in content or curriculum. But what was left for the public school? Control by the public and a curriculum informed by the common faith. Pioneer public educators, such as Horace Mann and Henry Barnard, sought through a judicious use of the Bible and other sources—including such civic documents as the Declaration of Independence—to preserve and pass on this common faith. The Reverend William H. Ruffner, Presbyterian minister, educated under William Holmes McGuffey, one-time chaplain at the University of Virginia,

[24]The Seventh Yearbook of The John Dewey Society is entitled *The Public Schools and Spiritual Values, op. cit.*, and one chapter is devoted to "The Origin, Development, and Validity of Spiritual Values."

[25]*Moral and Spiritual Values in the Public Schools* (Washington, D.C.: National Education Association, 1951).

Virginia's first State Superintendent of Schools, and a man who is sometimes called the "Horace Mann of the South," maintained in a document entitled *The Public Free School System* that "The State may formally teach the recognized morality of the country, and the will of God as the standard and ultimate authority of all morality, but distinctively religious teachings shall be left to volunteer agencies. . . ."[26] Such views, like those of Mann and Barnard, came close to embodying the theology of the founding fathers.

The Protestant leader Josiah Strong reflected similar views when he argued that the public schools should teach "the three great fundamental doctrines which are common to all monotheistic religions," that is, *"the existence of God, the immortality of man and man's accountability."* These are not sectarian, Strong maintained, and the public schools are "not Protestant, because *distinctively* Protestant doctrines are not taught in them."[27] Strong's "three great fundamental doctrines" are those of the eighteenth century Deists and of the founding fathers. They are not distinctively Protestant, but are they sectarian?

Some perceptive Catholic prelates argued that such teachings are sectarian. "Take away the distinctive dogmas of the Catholics, the Baptists, the Methodists, the Presbyterians, and so on," said Bishop Hughes of New York in the early 1840's, " and you have nothing left but deism," and deism is sectarian because it is not shared by all Americans.[28] "There is and there can be no positive religious teaching where the principle of nonsectarianism rules," asserted Archbishop Ireland in his famous address to the National Education Association in St. Paul in 1890.[29] He argued instead for a cooperative arrangement in which the public or "state" schools would engage in "secular" instruction and the religious schools in religious instruction.

William Torrey Harris recognized the difficulty involved in attempting to teach some sort of nonsectarian religion. "When we come to teaching a live religion in the school," he asserted, "we see that it must take a denominational form. . . ." Deism, far from being nonsectarian or neutral, is actually "opposed to all the creeds of Christendom." Harris concluded, then, that the public schools should be completely secularized.[30]

---

[26] As quoted in Sadie Bell, *The Church, The State, and Education in Virginia* (Philadelphia: The Science Press Printing Co., 1930), p. 438. Ruffner became State Superintendent of Schools in Virginia shortly after the Civil War. He wrote this document while in that position.

[27] Strong, *op. cit.,* pp. 95-98.

[28] As quoted in William Kailer Dunn, *What Happened to Religious Education? The Decline of Religious Teaching in the Public Elementary School, 1776-1861* (Baltimore, Md.: The Johns Hopkins Press, 1958), p. 254.

[29] As quoted in W. D. P. Bliss, *The New Encyclopedia of Social Reform* (New York: Funk & Wagnalls Co., Inc., 1908), p. 1056f.

[30] "The Separation of the Church from the Tax-Supported School," *Educational Review,* XXVI (October 1903), pp. 231-232.

What is sectarian and what is nonsectarian? The question has emerged frequently in discussions and court decisions about the use of the Bible in the public school. Catholics have pointed out the obvious: that the devotional or semidevotional use of the King James version is sectarian. Numerous others, from Mann on, have argued that the Bible, judiciously used, is nonsectarian, or that some portions of the Bible are not sectarian. Regulations for the use of the Bible in the public school have often provided that various versions could be used. The courts have been, and continue to be, divided on the question of the sectarian nature of the Bible. One of the early decisions which declared the use of the Bible in the public school to be sectarian was that of the Supreme Court in Wisconsin in 1890. "We cannot doubt that the use of the Bible as a textbook in the public schools, and the state reading thereof in such schools, without restriction, has a tendency," that Court declared, " to inculcate sectarian ideas, and is sectarian instruction. . . ."[31] Professor Donald Boles has pointed out that the highest courts of fourteen states have taken "an expressly favorable view of Bible reading in their public schools" whereas the "high courts of seven states . . . and a federal district court in Pennsylvania . . ." have held that such reading "violates either constitutional or statutory provisions."[32] The Supreme Court of the United States considered this question in the case of *Abington School District* v. *Schempp*.[33] Much of the testimony in the *Schempp* trial had to do with whether the Bible is a sectarian book. The Court's decision, which held that use of the Bible in a devotional or semidevotional fashion is unconstitutional, was based on the First Amendment which says nothing about sectarianism but provides that "Congress shall make no law respecting an establishment of *religion*. . . ." (Emphasis added.) Thus the question has shifted slightly, but importantly, from one meaning of "sectarian" to the meaning of "religion." It would appear that not only is the devotional use of the Bible questionable, and indeed declared to be unconstitutional by the highest court in the land, but it is quite apparent that even the open teaching of Josiah Strong's "three great fundamental doctrines" is subject to grave doubts. But the basic questions faced by Mann and nearly every public educator since are still very much with us: What remains for the public school to inculcate in preserving and passing on the common faith? What can the public school do about what I have called religion B? And what, if anything, can be done about religion A?

Teaching of and About Religion

One observer has pointed out that "for more than a century the people of the United States have shown a consistent determination to achieve two

---

[31] 76 Wisc. 177, 199.

[32] Donald E. Boles, *The Bible, Religion, and the Public Schools,* 2d ed. (Ames, Iowa: Iowa State University Press, 1963), pp. 58, 107.

[33] 374 U.S. 203 (1963).

seemingly irreconcilable ends; one of them to keep sectarianism out of the public schools, and the other to keep religion in them."[34] The achievement of this second goal has been attempted through a variety of means, including Bible reading, the study of religion in various ways, and the inculcation of moral and spiritual values. R. H. Dierenfield found in 1960 that Bible reading was conducted in over 40 percent of the public schools in America.[35] What effect the *Schempp* decision has had on this practice is not known.

Beginning in 1913, "released time" has caught the imagination of various religious and educational leaders. This is a type of program which enables the churches to teach their own members through some kind of cooperative arrangement with the public school system. The National Council of Churches "considers the movement so important that it has established a separate Department of Weekday Religious Education to stimulate and coordinate efforts to spread and improve the system."[36] Statements in favor of this type of program have been made by such denominations as the Methodists, the Missouri-Synod Lutherans, the Presbyterian Church in the United States, and the Mormons. Leo Pfeffer, a student of released time, "does not feel it is too much to say that 'the Catholic Church today is the most vigorous and passionate defender of the released time principle.' "[37]

Released time has been widely debated. Serious questions have been raised about its legality and about its educational effectiveness. The Supreme Court of the United States has handed down two decisions involving released time practices: one in 1948 declaring the program in Champaign, Illinois, which involved the use of public school facilities, to be unconstitutional; the other in 1952 finding a program not involving public school facilities to be constitutional.[38]

Released time has been on the increase ever since its beginning. Various surveys of the extent of this practice show a growth from approximately 10 percent of the schools surveyed in 1930 to approximately 30 percent in 1960.[39]

Occasionally efforts have been made to develop a "common core" of religious beliefs which could be taught to all children. Such efforts have faced difficulties of two types: (1) Just what is the common core? In the area of religion, and especially religion A, what can finish the sentence, "All Americans believe . . "? (2) Efforts to develop a common core have sometimes bordered on the devotional, as was the case, for example, in the New York Board of Regents

---

[34]Payson Smith, "The Public Schools and Religious Education," W. L. Sperry, ed., *Religion in the Post-War World* (Cambridge, Mass.: Harvard University Press, 1945), p. 32.

[35]R. H. Dierenfield, *Religion in American Public Schools* (Washington, D.C.: Public Affairs Press, 1962), p. 51.

[36]*Ibid.*, p. 77.

[37]*Ibid.*

[38]*McCollum* v. *Board of Education*, 333 U.S. 203; *Zonrach* v. *Clauson*, 343 U.S. 306.

[39]Dierenfield, *op. cit.*, p. 79 and Chapter XIV.

prayer, the use of which was declared unconstitutional in the case of *Engel* v. *Vitale.*[40]

Teaching "about" religion has received increasing support in recent years. This approach has been endorsed by various committees and conferences sponsored by the American Council on Education. The Educational Policies Commission of the National Education Association affirmed that "the schools can teach objectively *about* religion without advocating or teaching any religious creed."[41] Knowledge gained from such teaching is essential to a full understanding of our culture, literature, art, history, and present stiuation. The Commission on Religion in the Public Schools of the American Association of School Administrators recently expressed approval of the study of religion in the public schools and called for the "production of material of the highest educational and technical excellence" to be used for this purpose.[42] Teaching about religion seems also to have the approval of a majority of the justices of the Supreme Court, as indicated in the opinions in the *Schempp* case.[43]

While teaching "about" religion seems to offer a fruitful approach, it too creates problems. Where and how is it to be done in the curriculum? Who is to do the teaching? Is it possible to achieve objectivity and maintain neutrality in this area? Dierenfield found that over 75 percent of the schools which responded to his inquiries indicated that materials were provided to classroom teachers to help in teaching about religion. Most of these materials appeared to have been developed outside the local school system. One wonders how objective and even how educationally sound they are. Dierenfield also found that most teaching about religion takes place in regularly offered subjects, and generally is quite incidental to those subjects. This practice seems to occur most frequently at the

---

[40]370 U.S. 421 (1962).

[41]*Moral and Spiritual Values in the Public Schools, op. cit.,* p. 77.

[42]*Religion in the Public Schools* (Washington, D.C.: American Association of School Administrators, 1964), p. 59.

[43]Justice Clark, writing for the Court, indicated that "it might well be said that one's education is not complete without a study of comparative religion or the history of religion and its relationship to the advancement of civilization. It certainly may be said that the Bible is worthy of study for its literary and historic qualities. Nothing we have said here indicates that such study of the Bible or of religion, when presented objectively as part of a secular program of education, may not be effected consistent with the First Amendment." (374 U.S. 203, 225.) In his concurring opinion, Justice Brennan stated that "The holding of the Court plainly does not foreclose teaching about the Holy Scriptures or about the differences between religious sects in classes in literature or history. Indeed, whether or not the Bible is involved, it would be impossible to teach meaningfully subjects in the social sciences or the humanities without some mention of religion." (Id. at 300.) And Justice Goldberg, in his concurring opinion, which was joined in by Justice Harlan, pointed out that on the basis of "opinions in the present and past cases" one could conclude that "the Court would recognize the propriety of . . . the teaching *about* religion, as distinguished from the teaching *of* religion in the public schools" (Id. at 306).

high school level and in social studies and English classes. No more than 20 percent of Dierenfield's respondents indicated that special units about religion were used in elementary schools.[44]

"Moral and Spiritual Values"

Since World War II there has been increasing discussion of the role of the public school in instilling moral and spiritual values. Perhaps the most influential statement on this subject came from the Educational Policies Commission of the National Education Association and the American Association of School Administrators in 1951. Among the formulators of this statement were such nationally known figures as James B. Conant and Dwight D. Eisenhower.

"Intelligent and fervent loyalty to moral and spiritual values is essential to the survival of this nation," the Commission asserted. The development of such values "is basic to all other educational objectives." Thus the public schools, the common schools of the American people, have "a clear mandate to continue and to strengthen their efforts in teaching the values which made America great."

What are these moral and spiritual values? They are the values which, "when applied in human behavior, exalt and refine life and bring it into accord with the standards of conduct that are approved in our democratic culture." They are the values which are shared by the members of all religious faiths," the values "upon which the American people as a whole have agreed to manage their individual lives and their corporate activities. . . ." Specifically the Commission discussed the following values:

1. The supreme importance of the individual personality, the inherent worth of every human being. . . . .
2. Moral responsibility
3. Institutions as servants of men
4. Common consent
5. Devotion to truth
6. Respect for excellence
7. Moral equality
8. Brotherhood
9. The pursuit of happiness
10. Spiritual enrichment

These are the values of the common faith, of what I have called religion B. The Commission regarded the teaching of these values as so important to the common welfare that "there must be no question whatever as to the willingness

----

[44]Dierenfield, *op. cit.,* Chapter IV and especially pp. 58ff.

of the school to subordinate all other considerations to those which concern moral and spiritual standards."

What about the relation of these values to religion A? Obviously these values are sanctioned by all the great religions, and this can and should be pointed out in the public school. But it is also obvious that the religions differ on the nature of the sanctions and the roots of these values. The public school can point out that these differences exist (can teach *about* religion), and can teach respect for those who hold differing beliefs, but the public school cannot take sides. It can only teach that which is held in common. And the Commission was confident that "However we disagree on religious creeds, we can agree on moral and spiritual values."[45]

Undoubtedly one will find an overwhelming sentiment for this type of position. Most Americans look to the public school to teach more than the three R's. These are essential because an educated people is essential to the functioning of a democracy. But the "fourth R"—what I have called religion B—is just as essential. Citizenship involves not only the ability to read and write (so that one can vote intelligently, follow the deliberations of elected representatives, and write to Congressmen) and the ability to add and subtract (so that one can file his income tax return); citizenship also involves loyalty to democracy, allegiance to the republic, membership in the community of faith, and devotion to the common faith.

Democracy as a Faith

There are some who feel that such a designation as "moral and spiritual values" is too bland to describe the faith that makes us one as Americans, the faith that is necessary to our destiny. Professor J. Paul Williams of the Department of Religion of Mount Holyoke College is apparently one of these.[46] He has argued passionately that democracy is a faith, a religion, and that its fervent inculcaltion in the schools is essential to our survival as a people. Williams points out that "a culture is above everything else a faith, a set of shared convictions, a spiritual entity." He distinguishes between *denominational* and *societal* religion, the former being those beliefs and practices shared by the members of a particular group or denomination and the latter being those shared by "the members of a whole society."[47] People often assume that "denominational religion . . . is the only kind of religion which exists," but, in reality, "every functioning society has to an important degree a *common*

---

[45] *Moral and Spiritual Values in the Public Schools, op. cit.,* pp. vi, 3, 6, 29, 33, 54.

[46] See especially his chapter on "The Role of Religion in Shaping American Destiny" in *What Americans Believe and How They Worship* (New York: Harper & Row, Publishers, 1952; revised, 1962). Quotations that follow are from the revised edition.

[47] *Ibid.,* p. 477.

religion. . . . Every viable state. . . is in fact based on a societal religion, on a set of values believed by the dominant group to be ultimate."[48] The United States is no exception. While we have separation of church and state, of denominational religion from the organs of government, we do not have separation of religion and state.

The "best single word to describe the societal faith of America, the *ideal* toward which" that faith aspires, is "democracy."[49] In these critical times, when, for example, we are confronted by the religious fanaticism of communism, "democracy must become an object of religious dedication. Americans must come to look on the democratic ideal . . . as the Will of God or . . . the Law of Nature."[50]

Williams does not advocate a blind Americanism or nationalism. The democratic faith transcends national boundaries. "Democracy is a way of life for all men," not just Americans. While we cannot escape nationalism, which is a potent reality in the world today, we should seek an expression of the democratic faith which transcends the nation.

This democratic faith is so important, says Williams, that it should be taught by churches and synagogues, and above all by "governmental agencies." And it should be taught "as religion."[51] The public schools, especially, should teach the democratic faith. Schoolmen might affirm that they already do so, but Williams finds two things lacking: metaphysical sanctions and ceremonial reinforcement. Democratic faith must be taught, he argues, as the very law of life (whether this law be understood in a supernaturalistic or naturalistic context), and ceremonials must be devised which (1) recall and glorify the values of the democratic faith, (2) appraise the present and the self in the light of these values, and (3) bring about a "rededication to living according to the standards sanctioned by these values."[52] The public school "must become a veritable temple for the indoctrination of democracy."[53] Thus Williams speaks in an articulate and thought-provoking way for the role of the public school as the established church which elicits devotion to the common faith.

Some Conclusions

There is an attractiveness as well as forcefulness in Professor Williams' position. It has the merit of recognizing the importance of religion B and the role of the public school with regard to America's "common faith." Furthermore,

[48]*Ibid.*, p. 478.
[49]*Ibid.*, p. 480.
[50]*Ibid.*, p. 484.
[51]*Ibid.*, p. 488.
[52]*Ibid.*, p. 410.
[53]"The Schoolmen and Religion," *School and Society*, LXX   (August 13, 1949), p. 97.

one might prefer his forthrightness to blander talk of moral and spiritual values. However, I find myself unwilling to go the whole way with Williams. It is well that students be exposed to the writings and experiences of the founding fathers, but it is also important that they learn to see these men as human and not as supermen or gods. It is well that one learn as a youngster the symbolic and ceremonial acts of patriotism, but it is also important that one realize that his nation enjoys no exemption from history—that it is not sacred in the sense of existing beyond the realm of change, or corruption and renewal, rise and fall.

The basic problem is this: How does one develop devotion to the tradition, the "common faith," without giving over to absolutism? Fortunately, the tradition itself has tended at its best to be "open-ended" or less than absolutistic. Justice Jackson recognized this when he wrote in the second flag salute case: "If there is any fixed star in our constitutional constellation it is that no official, high or petty, can prescribe what shall be orthodox in politics, nationalism, religion, or other matters of opinion or force citizens to confess by word or act their faith therein."[54] This leaves moving space for dissenters. It also is based solidly on the very nature of the religious position of the founding fathers themselves, a position which unequivocally acknowledged authority beyond the nation. Love of nation was certainly not eschewed by these men, but it was understood in the context of a wider devotion to the freedom and equality, the unalienable rights, of *all* men. In writing on behalf of the adoption of the Constitution in the First Federalist Paper, Alexander Hamilton appealed to motives of philanthropy as well as those of patriotism and by philanthropy he meant literally love of mankind. James Madison pointed out in his *Memorial and Remonstrance on the Religious Rights of Man* (1784) that "Before any man can be considered a member of civil society, he must be considered as a subject of the governor of the universe," and thus "every man who becomes a member of any particular civil society" must do so in such a fashion as to reserve or maintain his "allegiance to the universal sovereign."[55]

Thus the founding fathers were committed to a source of value and a standard of judgment beyond the nation. While most Americans have shared this commitment, there has been a constant temptation to identify nation with God, to regard as absolutely true one's own understanding of the democratic faith. This tendency may be moderated in the public schools by a recognition that Americans do not universally agree on religious and political views, and by an exposure to differences and even to unpopular dissent. This means handling controversial issues honestly and judiciously rather than assuming that all Americans agree on political and religious matters.

In this connection, it might be helpful if the schools gave more attention to the study of religion A. This could be one way of dealing with the reality of

[54]*West Va. State Board of Education v. Barnette,* 319 U.S. 624, 642 (1943).
[55]*The Complete Madison,* Saul K. Padover, ed., (New York: Harper & Row, Publishers, 1953), p. 300.

difference in America as well as with an element of substantial importance to American civilization. A review of the typical textbook in American history—typical up until very recent times, at least—indicates that religion A is generally relegated to the early sections of the book which deal with the Colonial period. Once the nation got underway apparently all the Puritans, Quakers, and Baptists died off, leaving only Americans. Possibly the Mormons might come in for brief mention in connection with the westward expansion, but one might well assume that religion A had little or nothing to do with the developing nation.

A similar review of textbooks dealing with life in America today discloses that religion A is either ignored or some sort of pious statement is made about Americans agreeing even religiously on what matters. This latter type statement may be a testimonial to the power of religion B; that is, perhaps Americans do tend to shade into varieties of quite indistinguishable gray on questions that matter most to them. It is doubtful, however, that this does justice to our actual condition. Father John Courtney Murray reminds us that beneath the relatively calm surface of civility in relations between Americans of various religious views the deep tides of religious warfare ebb and flow.[56] It becomes important to ask, then, whether domestic peace is enhanced by glossing over some of our most fundamental differences or by facing them. The answer seems obvious. The health of our democratic society depends upon learning to live with differences; and unless the schools can expose us to these differences—in a controlled, educationally profitable atmosphere—there is not much reason for optimism regarding domestic stability.

It is also evident that religious groups and leaders have a role to play in dealing with similarities and differences in points of view and thus in strengthening the fabric of democratic society. We need more efforts to come to grips with the relationship between religion A and religion B. There is a tradition going back to the eighteenth century, to the beginning of our nation, which is the democratic tradition and which can be called our common faith. The organized religious groups, and especially the spokesmen for these groups, have devoted too little attention to examining the implications of this tradition for their own religious faith, and the relationship between their own particular religious positions and the common faith. In fact, this tradition has forced an openness upon the religious groups, the implications of which are not fully realized. At the same time, religion A can be a check on the excesses of religion B by a constant reminder of the reality of an authority beyond nation and by insisting upon the full right to believe in a particular religious point of view even though it is not shared by the majority.

[56]"America's Four Conspiracies," in John Cogley, ed., *Religion in America* (New York: Meridian Books, Inc., 1958), pp. 12-41.

Annotated Bibliography

American Council on Education, *The Relation of Religion to Public Education; The Basic Principles.* Washington, D.C., 1947.

Beman, Lamar T., *Religious Teaching in the Public Schools.* H.W. Wilson Co., New York, 1927. Bibliography and excerpts of significant materials from the Civil War to the early 1920's.

Boles, Donald E., *The Bible, Religion, and the Public Schools* 2d ed. Iowa State University Press, Ames, Iowa, 1963. Treatment of relevant state and federal court cases; also a discussion of attitudes of religious bodies.

Brickman, William W., and Lehrer, Stanley, *Religion, Government, and Education.* Society for the Advancement of Education, New York, 1961. Suggestive essays and useful documentary material.

Dewey, John, *A Common Faith.* Yale University Press, Inc., New Haven, Conn., 1934. Dewey's classic work on religion now issued as a Yale Paperbound.

Dierenfield, R.H., *Religion in American Public Schools.* Public Affairs Press, Washington, D.C., 1962. Based on a questionnaire study.

Douglas, William O., *The Bible and the Schools.* Little, Brown and Company, Boston, Mass., 1966. P. 59. Justice Douglas speaks for "a civic and patriotic heritage that transcends all differences among people, that bridges the gaps in sectarian creeds, that cements all in a common unity of nationality, and that reduces differences that emphasis on race, creed and sect only accentuate."

Drouin, Edmond G. (ed.), *The School Question: A Bibliography on Church-State Relationships in American Education, 1940–1960.* The Catholic University of America Press, Washington, D.C., 1963.

Duker, Sam, *The Public Schools and Religion; The Legal Context.* Harper & Row, Publishers, New York, 1966. Excerpts and brief summaries of most important U.S. Supreme Court Cases.

Dunn, William Kailer, *What Happened to Religious Education? The Decline of Religious Teaching in the Public Elementary School, 1776-1861.* The Johns Hopkins Press, Baltimore, Md., 1958.

Freund, Paul A., and Ulich, Robert, *Religion and the Public Schools.* Harvard University Press, Cambridge, Mass., 1965. The Burton and Englis Lectures for 1965. Professor Freund offers a succinct and perceptive treatment of "The Legal Issue." Professor Ulich's discussion of "The Educational Issue" is provocative.

Mead, Sidney E., *The Lively Experiment, The Shaping of Christianity in America.* Harper & Row, Publishers, New York, 1963. A most perceptive study.

National Education Association, *Moral and Spiritual Values in the Public Schools.* Washington, D.C., 1951.

Nielsen, Niels C.,Jr., *God in Education; A New Opportunity for American Schools.* Sheed & Ward, New York, 1966. Calls for more emphasis on teaching about religion in the public schools.

Sizer, Theodore R. (ed), *Religion and Public Education.* Houghton Mifflin Company, Boston, Mass., 1967. Seventeen papers presented before a Conference on the Role of Religion in Public Education at Harvard University. Legal and constitutional, historical and cultural, religious and secular aspects of this issue are examined in depth.

Stokes, Anson Phelps, and Pfeffer, Leo, *Church and State in the United States.* Harper & Row, Publishers, New York, 1964. A one volume abridgement and revision of the definitive three-volume classic which was published in 1950.

CHAPTER 3

Philosophy and Inquiry

W. Eugene Hedley

W. Eugene Hedley is an Assistant Professor of Philosophy of Education at the State University of New York at Stony Brook. He is author of the recently published book, Freedom, Inquiry, and Language: A Study in Three Contemporary Philosophies and Education. *He is currently working in the areas of philosophy of language and education and the philosophical bases of decision-making in education.*

We are like Mitya in *The Brothers Karamazov* — "One of those who don't want millions, but an answer to their questions"; we want to seize the value and perspective of passing things, and so to pull ourselves up out of the maelstrom of daily circumstances. We want to know that the little things are little, and the big things big, before it is too late; we want to see things now as they will seem forever—" in the light of eternity".[1]

If there is one thing that characterizes the younger generation of today — those young people now in our secondary schools and colleges — it is that they don't want millions, but an answer to their questions. There exists a pressing need among this group to orient themselves, to find a meaning for their lives in the midst of a rapidly changing society. Philosophers, since earliest times, have sought answers to this very sort of question, and while their answers have not always been convincing, the methods that they have demonstrated in dealing with the problems are and have been of immense value to the development of western culture.

Willis Moore in introducing a recent issue of *Educational Theory* states:

[1]Will Durant, *The Story of Philosophy* (*Time* Reading Program, special edition) (New York: *Time,* Inc., 1926), p. 1.

The purpose of this issue of *Educational Theory* is to present the case for a certain proposed innovation in the curriculum of our high schools. The proposal, made sporatically by individual teachers from the last decade of the last century down to the present, and officially though cautiously by a special committee of the American Philosophical Association in 1958, is that philosophic content be introduced into the programs of selected high school students.[2]

The purpose of this present chapter is to raise some questions concerning the assumptions behind the innovations described in this fascinating issue of *Educational Theory* and to suggest a somewhat different role for philosophy in secondary education. In short, I propose to consider this matter from the point of view of a philosopher of education, rather than from the point of view of either philosopher or teacher.

First, let me turn to the consideration of some of the assumptions made concerning the introduction of philosophy into the high school curriculum and raise some questions concerning their merit. Although it may seem to be a trite and even meaningless question, the question, "What is philosophy?" is one that carries considerable implication for those who propose to transfer philosophy from one type of educational institution to another. Let me pose some of the questions subsumed under this question in order to clarify the kinds of answers that might be appropriate. (1) Is philosophy to be equated with the body of written works of the philosophers of the past? Or, perhaps, a better question would be: Is the goal of philosophic studies the acquisition of the philosophic thought of the past? (2) Is philosophy to be equated with the content of the philosophy courses offered at the colleges and universities? (3) Is philosophy to be equated with a method or methods which can be termed "philosophizing" and if so, is the study of the works of the philosophers of the past and is the acquisition of such works or the matriculation through a series of courses in philosophy both a necessary and sufficient condition for being able to philosophize?

Another assumption directly related to the above has to do with the question of who *can* philosophize or *do* philosophize. Subsumed under this question are the following: (1) Are all human being philosophers at varying levels of sophistication? (2) Does this include adolescents? (3) If philosophy is considered synonymous with a method or methods of philosophizing, then is this method some skill to be acquired or is it a process natural to human beings which may be refined? In other words, is there a way to teach and/or improve this process in all individuals or is it a basic property of those persons of high intellect?

Still another assumption involves the issue of the value of philosophy. Again, Willis Moore offers us a summary:

---

[2]Willis Moore, "Philosophy in the Curriculum of the High School: Purpose and Plan of this Issue," *Educational Theory*, Vol. 17, No. 3 (July 1967), p. 203.

When these teachers get down to cases they insist on the same values for philosophy in the high school curriculum as have long been claimed for it in the college level of education. Philosophy properly taught engenders a reflective, critical and evaluative attitude in the student. Moreover it tends to produce breadth of perspective and induce humility in the practitioner. Where these attitudes are directed to the accepted and proposed answers to the big questions, there is less likelihood of frozen positions on the issues, a greater chance that new outlooks, new hypotheses, will be generated and tried out in the face of novel situations; and the high school age is none too early for the initiation of such attitudes.[3]

A consultation of the curriculum guides of most school districts would reveal the same values claimed for courses in mathematics, science, history, etc. Of course, it can be claimed that while these values may be realized in other courses, philosophy is the most appropriate means to achieve these values. But, what evidence do we have for this? I for one have found during my years as an undergraduate and graduate student in philosophy any number of competent and first-rate philosophers who certainly were not noted for their humility nor for their breadth of perspective. This, of course, is to say nothing much at all, for the real issue has to do with what is meant by "properly taught". Also, if it is desirable to evaluate the results of a particular subject matter, it is well to limit the claims for the value of such a course in such a way as to provide an objective which can be adequately analyzed and can provide some clues as to its proper evaluation.

Having raised some questions concerning assumptions as to the nature of philosophy, the nature of the philosopher, and the value of philosophy, herewith are suggested some answers that deviate from those which are assumed in many reports concerning the teaching of philosophy in the high school.

First of all, I would maintain that the nature of philosophy has much less to do with the writings of great philosophers than with a method of attack or method of inquiry into basic human problems. This is not to deny that the college curriculum in philosophy is not essential for the preparation of those individuals who would teach philosophy in the high school, for in no other way except through the formal subject matter of philosophy can an individual compare and analyze the methods of problem solving or inquiry that are employed in such divergent areas as science, social sciences, and the humanities.

However, the question remains as to what exists in the nature of philosophy that would make it valuable for the high school student. Certainly, it must be that of providing him with a method of attack upon basic human problems. Here it must be insisted that by "basic problems" the problems that are basic to the student are being referred to, rather than those problems that are deemed basic in the eyes of the great philosophers. The analysis of the student's

[3]Moore, "Summary and Defense," *op. cit.,* p. 266.

basic problem may well end up in one of the categories of basic problems dealt with by leading philosophers, but it is by no means necessarily the case.

Perhaps a few words need be said describing the particular view of philosophy taken here. To speak of philosophy as "philosophical method" is to describe what persons do as philosophers rather than to describe the product of their efforts. It is not only much in vogue to describe such activity as "analysis," but there is much justification in doing so - provided the nature of analysis is properly delineated. Philosophic method may be characterized by two forms of analysis. The first form is that of logical analysis. Logical analysis is concerned with analyzing the struture of linguistic forms so as to reveal and "draw out" the deductive inferences implicit within them. It also provides a meta-logical analysis, that is to say, an analysis of the nature of deductive systems themselves. Logical analysts are concerned with matters of validity, consistency, deductive procedures, and analyzing the meanings of ordinary propositions into logical categories amenable to deductive operations and criteria.

The second form of analysis is not so easily described nor labeled. Still, it is the form most essential to the education of any human being – using "education" in the finest sense of that term. This is also the form or method of philosophizing available and most important to each individual in determining his own life. To describe this method of analysis, what it "is" must be closely contrasted with what it "is not."

First, consider this form of philosophical analysis as a form of inquiry! But not like inquiry in a scientific sense, for inquiry in science sets out to discover something that has been hitherto unknown or unobserved. The scientist takes something apart, or analyzes it, in order to discover previously hidden causes or elements. On the other hand, philosophical inquiry or analysis is not concerned with the discovery of something new or hidden, but rather with viewing something already known and observed from a different perspective. Nothing external is found or discovered but, internally, an individual sees the old in a "light" previously unnoticed by him, although it was always there to see. For example, human beings have come to be viewed in an ever increasing number of perspectives: biologically, neurologically, psychologically, sociologically, politically, economically, morally, etc. This list along with the refinements of these categories show no indication that their number will not continue to multiply. Philosophical inquiry would apply itself to the clarifying of these views of man; clarifying them in the sense of increasing the awareness of the implications of each of these views or perspectives for human life in general as well as their implications for the other perspectives.

Now, while philosophical analysis is not concerned with discovery in a scientific sense, it does contain possible ramifications for discovery used in an internal, personal, and psychological sense. An excellent example of this is given by John Wisdom:

However, suppose now that someone is trying on a hat. She is studying it in a mirror. There's a pause and then a friend says, "My dear, the Taj Mahal." Instantly the look of indecision leaves the face in the mirror. All along she has known there was something wrong with the hat, now she sees what it is. And all this happens in spite of the fact that the hat could be seen perfectly clearly and completely before the words "Taj Mahal" were uttered. And the words were not effective because they referred to something still hidden like a rabbit in a hat. To one about to buy false diamonds the expert friend murmurs, "Glass," to one terrified by what he takes to be a snake the good host whispers, "Stuffed." But that's different, that's news. But to call a hat the Taj Mahal is not to inform someone that it has mice in it or will cost a fortune. It is hardly to say that it's like the Taj Mahal; plainly it's very unlike and no less unlike now that this far-fetched analogy has been mentioned. And yet nothing will undo the work of that far-fetched allusion. The hat has become a monument and too magnificent by half.[4]

Philosophical analysis or inquiry may serve an individual in a manner analogous to the uttering of "Taj Mahal." The "far-fetched analogy" in the hands of an individual adept at philosophizing can bring another, or himself, to see that which because of its very obviousness was overlooked before.

Thus, the important and perennial questions of philosophy, "What is truth?" "What is beauty?" and "What is good?" are not be viewed as questions for which we are to seek an answer in the sense that the scientist seeks for answers to his questions. Rather, they are to be viewed as analogies that serve to force us to review or to look afresh at the kinds of meanings that are attributable to a familiar concept or that are relevant to a particular issue or problem. In a psychological sense, these sorts of questions serve to prepare an individual to consider a modification of a familiar concept, for a fresh perspective shows as nothing else the limitations of the old.

The Function of Philosophy As Inquiry

From an educational point of view it may be said that philosophy, considered as analysis or a form of inquiry, has two functions. First, logical analysis at the linguistic level serves to draw formal distinctions which enable the individual to formulate clear and intelligible justifications for what he has come to believe as well as to critically analyze the justifications of others. Second, philosophizing or analyzing in the second sense presented here serves to aid the individual in reviewing and bringing to light the various meanings

[4]John Wisdom, *Philosophy and Psycho-Analysis* (Oxford, England: Basil Blackwell, 1964), p. 248.

involved in a concept or issue of which he has failed to be aware or which is in need of a new focus. This philosophizing also provides the individual with the opportunity to modify, enlarge, or change the meaning or meanings that he perceives in a concept or an issue.

To the question, "Who can be a philosopher?" or "Who can philosophize?", I must answer that this activity is open to all persons. Even more, not only can all persons philosophize, they *do* in fact philosophize. A person cannot exist in today's world without having his perspective, his world view, constantly altered, sometimes enlarged, and even changed. The aim of presenting philosophy in the high school would be to increase the level of sophistication with which an individual will come to carry out his philosophizing. All human beings, adolescents included, are confronted daily with basic issues, problems, and concepts. They invariably form some generalized notions concerning these problems and from these generalized notions extract still further general premises out of which a world view is continually being formed and shaped. Not only can all philosophize, but I would be so bold to suggest that those who could profit most from high school philosophy would be those of modest and low intellectual capacity as well as the emotionally immature. The bright and mature student in high school can look forward to four or more years of college education in which methods of dealing with problems will be presented in abundance. Moreover, one of the criteria by which intelligence is judged is by problem-solving ability. Thus, those students who will not be going to college are those most in need of having some experience in viewing problems from a variety of perspectives.

Problem Solving and "Vital Issues"

The values of philosophy too often contain "all of Heaven and Earth and then some." If a role is to be considered for philosophy in the high school curriculum, then it would seem appropriate to limit the claims to one that is both appropriate and realizable. What is being asserted in this chapter is that philosophy, viewed as analysis or as a specialized form of inquiry, can provide an approach to dealing with issues and problems which are of vital concern to the adolescent, and that this approach can make a significant addition to the education of all youth.

Assertions of and by themselves are all too easy to come by, so permit me to present an example of exactly how a high school course in philosophy might deal with a "vital issue." A serious problem confronting most high school students today and a problem with which they are vitally concerned is the issue of the smoking of marijuana. Furthermore, this is an issue about which many will be required to make a real decision at one time or another. The high school student may come to the philosophy class with this basic question: "Shall I, if given the opportunity, smoke marijuana?" What they expect from any teacher is, of course, an answer: "Yes" or "No." Unfortunately, the nature of our school systems has itself reinforced this expectancy on the part of students. They expect the teacher to provide an answer to all their questions. But, what the teacher of philosophy should be concerned with is the analysis of the question itself. The teacher should assist the students in deciding the methods or method appropriate to reaching a conclusion. As John Dewey said, "Above all, however, it should be made clear that the question is not what to do, *but how to decide what to do.*"[5]

The first step in coming to grips with "how to decide what to do" is to lead the students to a point where they are able to recognize that the question of whether or not to smoke marijuana is not a single question nor a simple one. The student should come to see that the question is first of all a scientific one; that is, it is a question of scientific data concerning the physiological and psychological effects of marijuana smoking. Students should then be directed to the collection of this data, not only from printed sources such as periodicals, newspapers, etc., but also from reports through other news media such as television; and then, once data concerning the physiological and psychological effects of marijuana are accumulated, the students should be confronted with the problem of how to evaluate this data.

A second dimension of the same problem is that of the legal aspects of marijuana smoking. Students should discover what the law actually says concerning the smoking of marijuana, what the legal penalties are for smoking marijuana, but more, they should seek to discover the process by which such laws come into being and then possibly an inquiry into the role of law itself in a democratic society. In short, students should be able to answer the questions: "What is the law concerning marijuana?" "How did these laws come to be passed;" and "What is the role of law in a democratic society?"

But the scientific and legal aspects of marijuana smoking are just the beginning, for the truly basic aspect of the question is a moral one. After determining and evaluating the scientific evidence relevant to marijuana and to the legal status of marijuana smoking, the basic question that the adolescent must still ask is "Ought I to smoke marijuana?" and the "ought" here can be seen in several dimensions. First, what is my obligation or the limits of my obligation to this or any other law? Second, what is my obligation toward myself in terms of preserving my physical and psychological well-being? Third, what are my obligations to the social mores of my community, my family, and would these obligations be affected were I to indulge in the practice of smoking marijuana?

It will be noted that in connection with this particular problem there has

[5] John Dewey, "Teaching Ethics in the High School," reprinted in *Educational Theory*, Vol. 17, No. 3 (July 1967), p. 223.

been no literature nor textbook prescribed. This is not to indicate that such a course must not contain these elements, but it should indicate that the teacher should be competent enough to bring or direct students to those materials which are relevant both to the problem under analysis and to the interests and capacity of the students. Some students may be capable of reading some of the philosophical analyses of "ought" presented in contemporary philosophical literature. Others may get insight into the nature of obligation either through readings in literature or through discussion of current motion pictures or television drama. The problem of obligation is indeed basic, so basic that philosophy has never maintained exclusive right to this issue and it appears throughout the history of literature as well as philosophy.

The question is often raised concerning the emotional maturity of students and how this might affect their ability to inquire into vital issues. Certainly issues as important and controversial as that of marijuana must give the teacher pause. However, I am quite sure that no competent teacher would ever think of taking the emotionally immature student into a controversial area without first laying the groundwork to insure the student's ability to deal with the subject at an appropriate level and in a proper perspective.

With this in mind, I would suggest as a prerequisite to the kind of philosophy course suggested by the above unit an intensive unit on logic and language. The emphasis here again would not be on duplicating (even at a "watered-down" level) a college course in introductory logic. Rather, I would select from the general areas of logic and language those concepts and those exercises which are directly relevant to carrying out at the high school level the type of inquiry described above. For example, students would be greatly aided in their analysis by being able to distinquish between truth and validity, between argument and emotional appeal, and between statements of fact, statements of value, statements of analysis, and statements of definition. They should understand some of the principles of general semantics; particularly, that the meaning of a word is more often revealed by how it is used than by what is said about it. In short, enough logic and language analysis should be provided to establish in the student a frame of mind in which inquiry into moral and ethical issues can be pursued in a more dispassionate and less threatening (to the student) manner.

What is being proposed, then, is first of all that a teacher well trained in philosophy is an ideal person to conduct this kind of philosophic inquiry – whatever it might be named – at the high school level. The course would have as its objective the assistance of students in acquiring a philosophic approach to inquiry by means of an analysis of those problems which are important to the student. It would be a course relevant to all students and, if possible, more relevant to those students who may not continue their education beyond high school. It would be a course in which the demanding questions of the younger generation would not be met directly, but would be met indirectly by leading them toward the development of ever more sophisticated approaches by which they can discover their own answers. The students in our high schools today, regardless of an increasing sophistication, are still more or less immature; and even though the basic concerns dealt with by the philosophers of the Fifth Century B.C. may be seen by contemporary philosophers to be relevant to the basic issues of today, it is a mistake to expect modern high school students to appreciate this relevance for the ability to appreciate such relevance is one of the things we mean by maturity.

In face of renewed interest and efforts toward the introduction of philosophy courses into the curriculum of our secondary schools, I feel compelled to reiterate those things which are *not* being recommended in this present paper. First of all, it is not being recommended that a "watered-down" version of a college philosophy course be included in the high school curriculum. Even though such a course would be of undoubted benefit to selected high school seniors, the fact remains that our secondary curriculum is already overloaded with necessary and desirable offerings – expecially for the college-bound student. The addition of one more "college-type" course hardly seems justified at this time.

It also should be understood that I am by no means convinced that all students should be philosophers. In other words, I do not believe that the content of the discipline of philosophy as represented by the content and procedures of courses offered at the college and university level are fully relevant to all secondary students. I am rejecting the value of the works of the great philosophers for all high school students – or at least I am rejecting their value as sufficient to warrant their inclusion in the curriculum.

Also, I would like to emphasize exactly what it is that has been recommended in the preceding pages. First, I feel strongly that somewhere in the secondary curriculum there should be a place where student problems – that is, problems that are felt by students to be immediate and important to them – provide the content for such a course or courses. Second, I feel that the method or approach employed in such a course or courses should be philosophical. This is to say that the method or procedure of such a course would not be designed to give answers to student problems, but rather to explore the methods which may be relevant to "deciding what to do." Third, I would hold that persons well trained in philosophy are most suited to assisting students in the analysis of or inquiry into problems from a philosophical perspective. Fourth and finally, the outcome of such a course or courses would be to increase the level of sophistication at which any and all students could deal with their own problems.

Annotated Bibliography

Beardsley, Monroe C., *Practical Logic*. Prentice-Hall, Inc., Englewood Cliffs, N.J., 1961. A classic work relating language analysis to logic.

Brown, L.M., *General Philosophy in Education.* McGraw-Hill Book Company, New York, 1966. Designed for student teachers and those in the later stages of their professional preparation. Part One, "Tools of Critical Thinking," is especially relevant to the discussion in the previous chapter.

Cohen, Morris R., and Nagel, Ernest, *An Introduction To Logic.* Harcourt, Brace & World, Inc., New York, 1962. A short introductory logical text now issued in paperback.

Copi, Irving M., *Introduction to Logic.* The Macmillan Company, New York, 1961. Part One deals with language. Chapter Two, "The Uses of Language," is especially relevant to the previous chapter.

Durant, Will, *The Story of Philosophy. Time* Reading Program, special edition, *Time,* Inc., New York, 1926. A basic introduction by the author of the Story of Civilization series.

Dewey, John, *How We Think.* D.C. Heath & Company, Boston, 1933. The book which prompted the problem-solving, critical thinking movement in social studies education.

Kerner, George C., *The Revolution in Ethical Theory.* Oxford University Press, London, 1966. A review and analysis of the contributions of G. E. Moore, Charles L. Stevenson, Stephen Toulmin, and R. M. Hare to the area of linguistic analysis.

Peters, R.S., *Ethics and Education.* Scott, Foresman & Company, New York, 1966. Critical philosophy—dedicated to clarification, systematic reflection, and rational argument—is the subject of this excellent book.

Scheffler, Israel (ed.), *Philosophy and Education.* Allyn & Bacon, Inc., Boston, 1958. The section on "Morals and Education" is relevant to the previous chapter. Chapters in this section are by C.L. Stevenson, Henry D. Aiken, and R.M. Hare.

Stevenson, Charles L., *Ethics and Language.* Yale University Press, New Haven, Connecticut, 1960. Stevenson's classic work on linguistic analysis now published in paperback.

PART III

Social Studies in a Mass Culture

The social studies have traditionally been held responsible for the training of good citizens. Even today, the National Council for the Social Studies has as its major objective the education of youth for desirable socio-civic behavior. At one time the term "good citizenship" referred in part to the education of immigrants in the American way of life. Good citizenship in social studies education has now come to mean the inculcation of proper values in all of the young. There is a general feeling of alarm among some for they contend that our industrial age has caused a breakdown in the home, church, and community. The school is expected to step into this void and make up for the abdication of other institutions. The responsibility of the social studies in this venture is obvious.

Yet, there is a good deal of confusion over key terms such as "democracy," "good citizenship," and "proper values." Agreement seems to be confined to the great faith all share in the ability of formal education to make the difference in young people's lives. Chapter 4 entitled "Democratic Schools or Schools in a Democratic Society" by Ronald E. Blood is most interesting for he candidly sifts the literature on democracy and education in order to give us a clearer picture of what the schools say they are doing compared to what the schools are actually doing. His findings are best stated in his own words as the reader will discover.

The advent of the industrial age in the United States can be clearly marked by the various myths which surround the term "bureaucracy." These myths are reinforced by what our social studies students learn from their parents—most of whom are employed by large organizations in our modern society. Students have also had first-hand experience with bureaucracies such as the organization from which they acquire their driver's licenses and the schools which they attend. One suspects, however, that our students have little understanding of the inner workings of bureaucracies, which is ironic in light of their future alliances with large organizations. Chapter 5 entitled "Organizations and Modern Society" by David P. Gardner is a very sophisticated account of bureaucracies in contemporary society. Implications for the social studies will be readily apparent to the reader.

The great faith Americans place in formal education is somewhat misplaced, for other institutions are extremely important in the lives of our social studies students. The importance of the mass media is understood by any parent who wakes up in the morning to his children's request for "funnies" on the TV. J. Herschel Parsons explores the political implications of the mass media in her chapter entitled "The Mass Media and Politics." As one's attention is drawn back to the primary objective held for the social studies, good citizenship, he realizes the relevance of this chapter for social studies education.

CHAPTER 4

Democratic Schools or Schools
in a Democratic Society

Ronald E. Blood

*Ronald E. Blood is an Assistant Professor of Educational
Administration at the University of California, Santa Barbara.
His study of the socialization of principals and teachers is
entitled* The Function of Experience in Professional
Preparation: Teaching and the Principalship. *He is presently
involved in an investigation of the organizational role of the
student.*

Practically from the inception of public education in this country, the schools
have been deemed the central institution for the promulgation of the nation's
democratic way of life. Public education, an American innovation, has
traditionally been held to be the pivotal point upon which the democratic
principle turned. An educated populace, and only an educated one, could wisely
govern itself, has been the American credo. If succeeding generations of
Americans failed to maintain a faith in and devotion to democracy, the schools
were and are to be held accountable by the public at large. The Credo is still
central to schooling in this country. Senator Kenneth Keating in his 1964
campaign remarked: "Education is the keystone of our representative
government. Far from being only a critic of our political life, it is, in a very real
sense the determinant of our ideals and their implementation." [1] Senator Robert
F. Kennedy in the same campaign said: ". . . it is the particular responsibility
of teachers of social studies to fortify the young in the attitudes and skills
needed for citizenship in a democracy and to educate them to make decisions
vital to the preservation of that democracy." [2] The charge given to the schools
by the public is clear and unequivocal.

The most continuous strand of heavy conflict in American education has

[1] *Social Science Record*, New York State Council for the Social Studies (Fall 1964), p. 1.
[2] *Ibid.*

been "how" not "whether" schools should serve as the pivotal institution of a democratic society. One current conflict in the language of educators occurs between professionals advocating an inquiry position for the social studies teacher and those advocating a good citizenship position. Partisans of either position though base their stand upon preparing individuals who will best sustain democratic principles. The inquiry partisans seem firmly committed to the position that by minimizing the teaching of values and maximizing the examination of values, the most desirable citizen for a democratic society will emerge. The good citizenship partisans appear to reverse the above position by maximizing upon the teaching of democratic values and minimizing examination of those values. By that process they, the good citizenship partisans, feel the most desirable citizen will emerge. Though oversimplified here the positions seem to resemble two equations with the same answer. The conflict does not appear to be whether schools are to educate students who will be most likely to contribute to a democratic way of life but rather upon how one goes about it. That is to say the pivotal nature of schools as public institutions is not, and has not, been challenged. The central nature of schools to a national way of life is assumed by the partisans. The partisans of both camps appear in that sense equally determined to produce good citizens. What they obviously differ on is not "whether" but "how" you go about it! Currently the social studies teacher is a focus for that conflict; but it has certainly swirled about the science teacher and the teaching of evolution, the English teacher and the teaching of literature. The continuing nature of the conflict has much to do with schools in a democratic society.

If the reader will abide for the time being with the position that the critical problem for schools and the social studies teacher is not whether they will actively engage in shaping citizens for a democratic society, but rather how they will go about it, it is necessary to examine the teaching of democracy and the assumptions made by current practice in schools and in the classroom. Schools by and large operate upon the progressive assumptions articulated by Dewey, that by doing one learns; that to experience, to take part in democratic procedures, is the best way to gain an understanding and commitment to those democratic principles. The evidence of the assumption rests in blossoming of student governments, in teachers being democratic, and in the seriousness surrounding classroom balloting on "what are we going to do today." John Dewey is cited as providing the rationale, the encouragement to schools to become democratic and to teach democracy through participation.

The social studies teacher of some few years' experience will recall that the involvement of students in the democratic process was only one aspect, one facet of the usage of the word democratic in schools, for teachers themselves were to be involved in the democratic process by democratic administrators in democratic schools. In recent years a cynicism has begun to evidence itself in the schools with reference to the use of the word democracy. Students have begun to reject participation in student government; and teachers, in some cases, seem uneasy about being treated democratically by school administrators. Students have become aware that in many cases balloting in a classroom meant confirming what the teacher had already decided to do and that freedom of the press did not necessarily apply to school newspapers. The growing cynicism with democratic procedures in schools presents a severe and critical problem for the very institution that society has assigned the role of being the keystone of representative government. The problem seems especially acute for the teacher of social studies.

The impetus of the progressive movement in education, styled in part as "learn by doing," provided, intentionally or not, the framework for teaching democracy by living it and experiencing it in schools. John Dewey succinctly states the position. ". . . we should take seriously, energetically, and vigorously the use of democratic schools and democratic methods in schools."[3] When arguments arose that classes taught by teachers could not really be allowed to rule by the majority vote, the response traditionally given was and is that majority rule was not the essence of democracy. If the argument was given that student governments could not really govern, the response was and is that democracy was and is something more than a form of government. Teachers found that democratic administration did not mean that the group decided an issue. The arguments given tend toward vagueness at best. An excellent example of that vagueness occurs in *Elementary School Administration*. The quotation follows from that recent (1967) textbook. "Democracy is an attitude. It is concerned with feelings and emotions — no form of organization or mechanical device can create a democratic organization."[4]

In order to discuss fruitfully the opportunities of experiencing democracy in schools as a prime method of teaching democratic principles, ideals, and values (a task clearly assigned to the schools), it is important and crucial to examine the usage of the term democratic by educators. What activities are described as democratic in schools? Democracy occurs with great frequency in the literature of education. It has been and continues to be a most popular adjective to describe schools, their purpose, and the activities occurring therein. Textbooks, speeches, and the private conversations of educators are replete with democratic ideals, democratic schools, democratic procedures, democratic classrooms, and democratic administration. The word is much overused in the writer's opinion, but the important point is not its overuse but the activities described or attributed to it by educators.

If, as practice indicates, students are expected to learn our government forms by experiencing them in schools, it is important not only to focus upon

---

[3]John Dewey, *Philosophy of Education* (Totowa, N.J.: Littlefield, Adams & Company, 1961), p. 38.
[4]Emery Stoops and Russell Johnson, *Elementary School Administration* New York: McGraw-Hill Book Company, 1967), p. 35.

the democratic activities we as educators engage them in, but also to focus upon those activities which the professional staff of the school engages in and describes as democratic. In other words, by discussing and examining how educators apply democracy to the organization of schools, the writer will deal with those sets of democratic procedures which teachers and administrators themselves experience.

In the textbook cited earlier, Stoops and Johnson argue, "The people must identify themselves with the organization. Democratic leadership is a process of helping others to help themselves in the alchemy of aims which have become intrinsic to them."[5] The foregoing statement does little to clarify the use of "democratic" for the helping relationship described as democratic would appear to apply equally well to the relationship obtaining between the psychotherapist and his clients or a father and his sons. The textbook quotation continues, "The principal who functions democratically delegates authority and responsibility to his staff." This portion of Stoops' and Johnson's remarks on democracy certainly describes normal bureaucratic structure; i.e., delegation of authority, but how democracy enters in seems quite unclear. The authors continue, "He (the democratic principal) consults with staff members for advice in their special areas of competence before making decisions." Agreed, this in all likelihood is desirable behavior, but again it is equally descriptive of a general of the army consulting with his staff before making a decision. Most individuals would be reluctant to describe the general as being democratic in his behavior.

Continuing from Stoops and Johnson, "He (the democratic principal) helps his staff to succeed and to look well while succeeding, then praises their success publicly and privately." Again, desirable behavior on the part of a school administrator or teacher, but how, in what way democratic? If we mean no more in schools than democratic behavior is something "good" and that when we use the word as an adjective — democratic leadership — we mean no more than to say something "good" that could suffice. On the other hand, it would seem that participants in the very institution which is to serve as the bedrock, the foundation of a democratic way of life, must question loose application of the word. What behavior is it that we wish students to understand as democratic? Is all "good" behavior democratic behavior? It does seem safe to assume that students will acquire some understanding of democracy by observing and participating in activities labeled "democratic." It is a prime thesis in this chapter that the current evidence of increasing cynicism toward activities styled as democratic procedures in schools, on the part of teachers, administrators, and students alike, is at least partially accounted for by their being engaged in activities and experiences labeled "willy-nilly" as democratic and which were, in fact, far from democratic.

The following few pages present something of a case study which is offered as an example of such an instance. The example centers upon the teacher being

[5]*Ibid.*

engaged in the democratic process in the hope of bringing home to the reader something which I strongly suspect students experience from grades K to 12.

The following quotation is abstracted from the 1955 Yearbook of the American Association of School Administrators. The rhetoric is offered here as an explanation of democracy in schools, though the example refers to school administrators, teachers will not find it difficult to recognize the classroom application:

> During its two years of work the Yearbook Commission has been guided by the belief that school administration must be a cooperative enterprise. If it is to be an effective cooperative enterprise, the administrator must be highly skilled in the art of managing and working with all kinds of people—his administrative and supervisory personnel, classroom teachers, students, and parents and other citizens who reside in his community. The Commission also believes that unless administration results in the improvement of teaching and learning, the main business of the schools, it will miss its greatest opportunity.
>
> Such convictions imply a leaning toward democratic school administration as opposed to the older concept of control based on power, status, and authority.[6]

In duscussing the above statement, I think it useful to (1) examine what the authors intended to communicate; (2) further examine what is communicated but perhaps not intended; and (3) explore the effect of the authors' position in an applied situation.

First, as to the intent of the authors: they state a belief that school administration must be a cooperative enterprise leaning toward democratic administration. The administration is viewed as "working with" citizens, teachers, students, parents, etc. Democratic administration is presented as being opposed to the older concept of control based on power, status, and authority. By being democratic the authors appear to imply that the administrator involves others ȋn the decision-making process. He tends not to use power, status, and authority to achieve goals, but rather "works with" groups, serves as a leader, and helps evolve decisions from groups, Rather than determining how things shall be, the democratic administrator listens to the opinions of the group; he assists the group in arriving at solutions to problems rather than imposing solutions to problems upon the group.

I think the foregoing is a reasonable interpretation of what the AASA authors intended to communicate to the reader. Now, to a consideration of what they communicated but perhaps did not intend.

The words used by the authors would appear to indicate that democratic administration is not based upon principles of power, status, and authority

[6]Yearbook of American Association of School Administrators (1955).

which they describe as being an older concept of control. As a reader, I am left somewhat puzzled, for to eliminate so much of human behavior I cannot conjure up a picture of any human organization in which these concepts are not basically operative. It is difficult to accept that the authors actually intended to picture democratic administration as being opposed to the older concept of control. Perhaps they only wished to communicate that they consider it bad form to openly utilize power, status, and authority. It would appear that these words, for the authors, carry a negative connotation; the word democratic carries a positive one, a good one.

There is evidence that such attitudes have been widespread in the field of education in the past and, to a considerable extent, in the present. If power, authority, and status are viewed as negative attributes, but at the same time are inherent in human organization, it is reasonable to expect that the former could come to be disguised or called by more acceptable names. Students, I suggest, soon learn that democracy in the classroom is indeed limited by the power, status, and authority of the teacher.

Teacher involvement in policy making has been a characteristic of what is styled as democratic administration. I would like to examine here a particular instance of such a case. A California State Department of Education publication reports a study on utilization of cumulative records. An increase in usage of such records was noted when teachers were involved in the policy-making process. It is interesting to note the conclusions drawn in the study. "The implications appear to be clear. To increase the use of cumulative records by teachers, it is important that the teachers be involved in policy decisions concerning the records. Many of the benefits derived from participation are plainly reflections of the effect on morale of having been a part of the process. Also, involving teachers in the policy-making process helps them become better aware of the many possible uses of records as well as some of the skills necessary for their proper use."[7]

It is important to note that at no point is mention made that teachers were included in the policy-making process because they had skills and knowledge appropriate to the solution of the problem or because they had a right to be so involved. Indeed, the increase in usage of records is attributed to higher morale.

Second, benefit obtained from their participation in policy making is reported as growth in the teachers' understanding and skills in cumulative record usage, not as more effective policy. It appears that democratic administration here involved teachers in the policy-making process (1) to derive better morale (make the teachers feel better) and (2) to provide in-service training which presumes insufficient knowledge on the part of the teachers.

I would maintain here that power, authority, and status were used in a

[7]L. H. Stewart and Arthur D. Workman, *The Students' Cumulative Record—Unachieved Potential* (Berkeley, 1961-1962) (Sacramento: California State Department of Education, 1963), p. 24.

manipulative manner. On the surface it would appear that the teachers were involved in order to help arrive at a better, more effective policy, but examination of the conclusions of the study belie this. One does not usually go to the less well informed for policy making; and in the case presented here, the administration presumed lack of knowledge and skill on the part of the teachers. If, however, his goal was not policy making, but morale and in-service training, his actions become more comprehensible. As a side issue, it would be interesting to know why the investigators did not consider the improvement in cumulative record usage a result of teacher knowledge and skill in policy development.

In summary, the point to be made is that democratic administration relies as much on power, status, and authority as any form of administration. The difference is that the concepts are likely to be used somewhat covertly and manipulatively. It is this covert usage which is apparent in the statement from the AASA Yearbook. What the authors intended to communicate was that democratic school administration is based on something other than power, status, and authority. It is my supposition that the "something other" is *covert* power, status, and authority. To test this supposition it is only necessary to take a democratic administration at its word and behave as if these concepts were not basic to the administration. Power, status, and authority will soon become apparent.

The example related to teacher involvement in democratic procedures would appear to apply equally well to student involvement. This suggests that students are frequently asked to participate in democratic procedures in order (1) to raise their morale, motivate them, make them feel good, and (2) to teach them something. Student cynicism may well be related to their recognition of the covert use of power, status, and authority. To convey to the student that democratic procedures are based on something other than power, status, and authority, that older concept of control seems quite strikingly different from conveying to them that democracy is a form of organization with a particular and distinctive distribution and arrangement of power, status, and authority.

So far in this essay I have suggested the following:

1. Schools are assigned the task of teaching democratic principles.
2. The most widespread curriculum belief is that one learns best by doing, experiencing democratic principles.
3. Schoolmen prefer to believe that schools themselves are democratic; hence schools provide an excellent base from which to experience democracy—teachers and students alike.
4. Teachers and students alike appear to be reflecting an increasing cynicism toward procedures styled democratic.
5. Further, I have suggested that the tendency of schoolmen, teachers, and administrators alike has been to define democracy in such a way that it can be used to describe most all desirable or good behavior.

John Dewey has made the best known attempt at relating democracy and education. It is to his work that I turn at this point in an attempt to explain current democratic practices in schools. Dewey remarked, "A democracy is more than a form of government; it is primarily a mode of associated living, of conjoint communicated experience." This led off in the same muddied stream of current definitions by educators but Dewey's next sentence seems especially distinctive. He continued, "The extension in space of the number of individuals who participate in an interest so that each 'has to refer' his own action to that of others, and to consider the action of others to give point and direction to his own."[8]

It is the "has to refer" which seems central to Dewey's definition of democracy and it is the "has to"; that is, the "must" portion which appears rather deliberately eliminated from more current definitions of democracy in schools. If Dewey's statement is to be applied, one then must look carefully at sets of interactions in school to see whether or not the participants "have to refer," "must refer" their own actions to that of others and vice versa. If the criterion holds, questions are raised such as, does a school faculty "have to refer" its actions to that of the student body and the student body to the faculty in order to give point and direction to their respective actions? It can and has been strongly argued that it "should be," "ought to be so" but one would be hard put I think to discover these "ought tos' " in practice. In practice the teacher "may" decide to refer his actions to that of the students and the school administrator "may" decide to consult his faculty on an issue. The teacher "may" decide to involve students in setting up rules and regulations for classroom behavior. The difference between "may" and "must" goes to the heart of the matter.

Dewey's definition of democracy has about it no air of permissiveness, and yet permissiveness appears to pervade those activities usually labeled as democratic in schools. The movement of teachers' organizations, increasingly militant, can be seen as rejecting the "may" relationship and insisting upon relationships characterized by "musts" — California's Winton Act which requires school boards to meet and confer with the representatives of teacher organizations serves as one example of a shift from "may" to "must." In Dewey's sense, the requirement of "meet and confer" can be said to be democratic as the arrangement is such that each group has to refer its actions to each other.

It seems that the application of the concept of democracy in schools, by schoolmen, refers only to the first portion of the statement quoted from *Democracy and Education:* "the extension in space of the number of individuals who participate in an interest. . ." (the more people involved the better). The

---

[8] John Dewey, *Democracy and Education* (New York: The Macmillan Company, 1930), p. 101.

latter portion of the quotation "so that each has to refer his own actions to that of others, and to consider the action of others to give point and direction to his own" seems to have been neglected — by teachers, administrators and students alike. If a student is to experience democracy in school both elements of Dewey's statement would need to be present — one alone is not sufficient unless we wish to convey to the student that participation alone describes democratic procedures without consideration of the right to participation. Participation by invitation is one thing; participation by right, quite another.

While the pivotal nature of schools in society has not been challenged, the concerns of the relationship of democracy to schools have changed. Consider the difference between democratic schools and schools in a democratic society. In the first case, schools are to be regarded as miniature democracies; in the second case, the focus is upon the arrangements made by a democratic society for its schools. In other words, it may be all too easy to confuse or fail to recognize the difference between using democracy as an organizing concept applied "externally" to schools and utilizing democracy as an internal organizational concept. The position of this essay is that educators have tended not to delineate the two applications or have drifted unwittingly from one application to the other.

The difference in the concerns of schoolmen with democracy and the schools in the past and in the present is evidenced on the one hand by Mann's concern for what I am describing as the external application of democracy as an organizing principle. Lawrence Cremin says of Mann: "The genius of Mann's design, and the hub of a built-in dynamism that has characterized American public education ever since, was the vesting of political control in the people. Through state legislatures and local boards of education, popularly-elected representatives rather than professional schoolmen would exercise ultimate oversight. The manifest reason was that public supervision must follow public support, and this, of course, was reason enough. Yet the relationship went far deeper. For by the artful device of lay control the public was entrusted with the continuing definition of the public philosophy taught its children."[9]

Mann's concern with democracy would appear to be somewhat different from the more current concerns with schools being miniature democracies. There is some amount of paradox in democratic arrangements intended to control schools (external application) and democratic arrangements for schools to control themselves (internal application), that is, a democracy within a democracy. The external-internal application of democracy as an organizing principle is delicate yet crucial to the question of "how" to educate for citizenship. It is critically important to examine the applications carefully in order to maximize upon the school setting in such a way as to avoid the cynicism growing out of mistaking paternalistic participation for democracy.

[9]Lawrence A. Cremin, *The Transformation of the School* (New York: Vintage Books, 1961), p. 10.

The sociologists Blau and Scott offer some purchase on the problem at hand through their development of an organizational typology referred to as "Qui-bono"? – who benefits?[10] Their typology consists of four organizational types, identified by raising the question, who benefits? The four types specified are (1) mutual benefit associations (a trade union); (2) business concerns, the owners being prime beneficiaries; (3) service organizations with the client as prime beneficiary; and (4) commonweal associations in which the public at large benefits. For each organizational type Blau and Scott suggest critical areas of control problems: a mutual benefit association must be able to insure internal democratic control if the membership is indeed to remain the prime beneficiary. The problem in the business concern is obviously different if the owners are to remain prime beneficiaries. If the client is to remain the prime beneficiary of a service organization, the practitioners as opposed to the managers must maintain control; and in the fourth type; the commonweal organization, the critical problem is maintaining external democratic control if the public is to benefit from its governmental agency.

The difficulty of placing schools in any single category is recognizable. "A public school, for example, benefits both the client group, i.e., the students, and the public at large. The problem here is whether to use as the basis of classification the short-run benefits as Blau and Scott did or the long-run benefits for which an equally strong case can perhaps be made."[11]

Teachers will readily identify the placement of schools as service organizations and the conflicts occurring between the needs of students and the needs of the organization, between teacher and administration. The classification of schools as commonweal organizations is also readily identifiable by the unceasing attempts of the public to maintain control over the schools, that is through legislation, school board elections, recall elections, disputes over textbooks, etc. Occasionally, one may even criticize schools as behaving like business organizations. The category in which schools appear least likely to fit is significantly the only category in the Scott-Blau typology in which internal democratic control is required, that is, the mutual benefit organization.

The "Qui-bono" typology is represented here in order to provide a conceptual framework within which to consider the application of democracy to schools. The difficulty of a "forced fit" for schools in the typology brings into focus the internal-external application of democracy as an organizational concept – internal for mutual benefit, external for the public at large. Democratic schools or schools in a democracy?

[10]Peter M. Blau and W. Richard Scott, *Formal Organizations* (San Francisco, Calif.: Chandler Publishing Co., 1962).

[11]Richard H. Hall, F. Eugene Haas, and Norman F. Johnson, "An Examination of the Blau-Scott and Etizian Typologies," *Administrative Science Quarterly* (June 1967) (Ithaca, N.Y.: The Graduate School of Business and Public Administration, Cornell University), pp. 119-120.

John Dewey articulates the position of schoolmen when he stated in 1932: "I think, that unless democratic habits of thought and action are part of the fiber of a people, political democracy is insecure. It cannot stand in isolation. It must be buttressed by the presence of democratic methods in all social relationships."[12]

The difficulties in implementing Dewey's position are quite important when the unit of organization is controlled by external democratic arrangements. The relationship of schoolmen to school boards serves as an example for analysis. The school board serves as a part of the formal arrangements for the democratic control of schools. Can the school board members, in turn, behave democratically in their relations with the schoolmen employed by them? If by "democratic" we abide by the proffered definition of Dewey, "The extension in space of the number of individuals who participate in an interest so that each 'has to refer' his own action to that of others and to consider the action of others to give point and direction to his own," if that definition is held to, then the internal-external paradox becomes singularly evident. It is most likely that the school board would fail to be democratic, fail in the sense that they would "have to attend to," "have to refer to" groups and individuals in the community at large but would necessarily revert to a "may attend to," a "may refer to" position with regard to individuals and groups within the school organization. The aggressive movement in teacher organization confirms, I suggest, this necessary arrangement. When teachers work for change from within as "faculties" the insufficiency of democracy as an internal organizing concept becomes evident. In essence, teachers through their extra-school professional organizations have entered into the external democratic process thereby becoming a part of the political interplay around school boards and state legislatures. By engaging in the democratic process (external) the teachers' organizations are then more likely to obtain a "has to refer" relationship with the school board or legislature, a relationship not available to them through democratic procedures (internal).

The social studies teacher, especially if involved in student governments, will recognize the difficulties presented by trying to maintain democratic procedures (internal) in a setting controlled by democratic procedures (external). Of late, students, too, have entered the external democratic arena even to the extent of operating off campus underground newspapers—a disconcerting event in democratic schools but not so disconcerting with regard to schools in a democratic society.

The disenchantment of students and teachers alike with procedures styled as democratic in schools must be taken seriously and especially so by the social studies teachers. This disenchantment is understandable if we as schoolmen have attempted to teach through contrived experiences that power, status, and authority are alien to democratic procedures as opposed to teaching that power,

---

[12] John Dewey, *Philosophy of Education, op. cit.,* p. 66.

status, and authority are distributed, arranged in a particular, distinctive fashion in a democracy. The disenchantment is also understandable if we have taught that democracy is participation as opposed to the right to participate or that the prime purpose of participation is related to boosting morale as opposed to better decisions.

The attempts at defining democracy are innumerable and voluminous. The few sentences quoted from Dewey's writings are not presented here as a sufficient definition of democracy. Dewey's writings on the subject consists of hundreds of pages, not a few sentences, but the few sentences quoted here, while not sufficient, are necessary to a working definition of democracy. The two elements contained in the statement provide a means by which to examine relationships among men. They are applicable to the school setting. Activities described as democratic can be examined, tested for the presence of (1) a broad base of participation and (2) a style of participation in which each "has to refer his own action to that of others, and to consider the action of others to give point and direction to his own."

The elements of this definition suggest something more complex than majority rule. To have to refer one's action to others does not infer that one must do as others say. On a national level, Senator William Fulbright of Arkansas would serve as an example. Senator Fulbright may not vote on a particular issue as his constituents would have him vote but he must refer that action to his constituents. On a local level, school board members are not free to act without referring those actions to the community. The public nature of school board meetings, along with the *requirement* that the only items which may be acted upon are those on a preannounced agenda, serves as evidence of the democratic arrangements in Dewey's sense.

In summary, I have attempted in this essay first, to bring about a focus on the school as a setting for teaching democratic procedures, principles. In doing so I have proposed that a distinction needs to be made by schoolmen between external democratic control (schools in a democratic society) and internal democratic control (democratic schools). The distinction is as necessary for students as it is for schoolmen. Second, I have proposed that it is necessary to distinguish between the "may participate" condition and the "right to participate" condition. Confusion between permissive behavior and democracy is especially unfortunate. Third, participation in democratic procedures is of a particular nature, that is to say it requires the referral of one's own action to that of others.

In concluding, when instances occur, and they occur often, in which democratic procedures (internal) are prevented or minimized by democratic procedures (external) rather than contriving or labeling activities as democratic, the teaching techniques of role playing or simulation would seem more appropriate. To role play or simulate democratic conditions avoids the misunderstanding on the part of students that the covert use of power is the essence of democratic procedures. Hopefully, schoolmen as well will examine their use of democratic procedures in the internal operation of schools.

Annotated Bibliography

Blau, Peter M., and Scott, Richard W., *Formal Organizations.* Chandler Publishing Co., San Francisco, Calif., 1962. A theoretical approach to understanding behavior in modern organizations.

Blood, Ronald E., *The Function of Experience in Professional Preparation: Teaching and the Principalship.* Unpublished doctoral dissertation, Claremont Graduate School, 1966. An inquiry into the socialization of school principals.

Cicourel, Aaron V., and Kitsuse, John I., *The Educational Decision-Makers.* Bobs-Merrill Company, Inc., Indianapolis, Ind., 1963. A research study conducted at Lakeshore High School in 1958 by two Northwestern University professors. There are chapters on the school as a mechanism of social differentiation, parental and student college aspirations, incoming Freshmen, counseling, high school bureaucracy, and social mobility. An excellent book on the decision-making process in high schools.

Cremin, Lawrence A., *The Transformation of The School.* Vintage Books, New York, 1961. The most definitive book yet published on the progressive movement in American education.

Dewey, John, *Democracy and Education.* The Macmillan Company, New York, 1930. Dewey's introduction to the philosophy of education. In many ways his best work.

Dewey, John, *Philosophy of Education.* Littlefield, Adams & Company, Totowa, New Jersey, 1961. Originally published under the title *Problems of Men.*

Stoops, Emory, and Johnson, Russell E., *Elementary School Administration.* McGraw-Hill Book Company, New York, 1967. A discussion of the many functions performed by elementary school principals.

Zeigler, Harmon, *The Political Life of American Teachers.* Prentice-Hall, Inc., Englewood Cliffs, N.J., 1967. The author argues that the world of education cannot be separated from the world of politics.

CHAPTER 5

Organizations and Modern Society

David P. Gardner

David P. Gardner is Assistant Chancellor and Assistant Professor of Higher Education at the University of California, Santa Barbara. His recent book, The California Oath Controversy, *was acclaimed by Professor Sidney Hook as ". . . a contribution of the first importance to the educational history of the United States."*

Our time is characterized by organized hugeness. Indeed, modern society is in large measure an organizational society[1]; that is, organizations process and control our essential functional needs: communications, transportation, education, defense, social order, recreation, justice, and matters of the spirit. The organization is the most powerful social unit of which modern society is comprised for it ministers rationally, effectively, and efficiently to man's dependency better than does any other social form. While it may be a god to some and a devil to others, the ubiquitous organization is a simple fact of social life for modern man and, in the main, the arena within which his claims for success, income, and security are resolved.

Organizations constitute society's principal mechanism for men co-operatively to provide for their joint and variegated needs and to protect themselves and their resources. They have as well a "pervasive influence upon individual and group behavior, expressed through a web of rewards, sanctions, and other inducements that range from patent coercion to the most subtle of group appeals to conformity."[2] The system of rules and norms by which this influence is in part manifested may be simple or highly complex depending upon the structure of the unit and the number and variety of its goals. Man's

---

[1] Robert Presthus, *The Organizational Society* (New York: Alford A. Knopf, Inc., 1962).
[2] *Ibid.,* p. 1.

acquiescence in, or perhaps more precisely, his assent to the system is explicitly understood to be exchanged for the benefits that only these huge social instruments of modern society can bestow. It is in a way a social compact, the implications of which carry impressive and sometimes frightening consequences for individual freedom and for the quality of life in our age.

Our society is geared to complex organizations and we vest in them heavy proportions of our faith, future, and fortunes, thereby becoming dependent on them. Organizational ineptitude or failure can have shattering consequences for individuals, communities,nation-states, and, in the instances of military defeat or economic disaster, for entire cultures. The decisive importance of the organization to the welfare of modern society, therefore, gives reason to the instrumental use of its members, not for their self-realization, but for their relevance to organizational objectives, power, and survival. The consequences of this relationship, which weighs rationality against human values on the scale of organizational purpose, are immense, to society if the organization stumbles or falls, and to the individual if his assent to the system is conditioned on the relinquishment of his freedom and happiness. Imbalance carries heavy social and human costs. The problem of modern organizations is thus "how to construct human groupings that are as rational as possible, and at the same time produce a minimum of undesirable side effects and a maximum of satisfaction."[3]

While it may be generally conceded that complex organizations are the most rational and efficient form of social grouping known, our understanding of them is limited and segmented. What little of them is understood is further fragmented owing to the biases brought to their investigation by the various social sciences. The organizational model for the political scientist, for example, implies bureaucratic power exercised to gain law and order in a given political unit or among such units. For the sociologist and historian, bureaucratization is the rationalization of collective activities, and for the economist corporate structure denotes the means for the arbitration and allocation of wealth, goods, and services. Each school, with its own terminology, points of reference, and bias, while providing some insight into how persons interact and how groups interact within organizations, yields relatively little useful information about the interaction of organizations with each other.

The interaction of organizations, on the other hand, even if more perfectly understood could not be regulated according to any single model, even in the most monolithic of societies. Yet, societies in their variety do differ from one another in the extent to which organizational interaction is regulated. The United States, for example, differs from most other modern societies "in the size of the sector of organizational interaction which is comparatively free of control or government regulation."[4] Britain and France, while regulating organizational

---

[3] Amitai Etzioni, *Modern Organizations* (Englewood Cliffs, N.J.: Prentice-Hall, Inc., 1964), p. 2.

[4] *Ibid.*, p. 111.

interaction more heavily than does the United States, practice a scope of regulation far narrower than do Communist societies where the most pervasive control over organization relations is asserted. To whatever extent government regulation is not manifested in organizational interaction, the pattern is dictated by the processes of conflict or cooperation, exchange or bargaining, "all of which are affected by ecological, cultural, and power factors."[5] The paucity of information and understanding of these processes, however, makes no less substantial the critical nature of the problem. Modern society, whose dependency on large-scale organization seemingly grows ever greater, tends to devise more and more instruments of regulation, ostensibly to encourage the rationality, effectiveness, and efficiency of organizations and man's happiness, freedom, and well-being within them. How well this process is understood and how efficaciously the balance is struck between organizational needs and human values will determine in substantial measure the quality of life in our society and the survival of our culture.

Factors in the Organizational Phenomenon

Organizations are not uniquely modern. By coordinating personnel with resources, however unevenly, societies have cooperatively from recorded history made provision for their several needs. The irrigation systems and the great wall of China, the pyramids of Egypt, the legions of Rome, the navy of Great Britain—all attest in ancient through medieval times to organized, collective activity on a gigantic scale. But these organizations were few in number and encompassed relatively small numbers of the total population of those societies. In contrast to earlier times, contemporary society has put a premium on rationality, effectiveness, and efficiency. These attributes are the *raison d'être* for modern organizations. The contemporary social environment, owing to radical changes in the nature of society—secularization, urbanization, industrialization, politicization—is both hospitable to large-scale organizations and dependent on them for its functional requirements. What characterizes the modern organization as against its antecedents is not so much its bewildering complexity as its rationality and efficiency. It is these modifications in the service of old functions, not the emergence of new functions, that distinguishe contemporary organizations and give them their uniqueness. Amitai Etzioni has made clear that "small, simple societies fulfill the same basic social functions as large, complex ones."[6] Each produces goods, services, and wealth, however crudely; each allocates human and material resources, however unjustly; and each realizes social and normative integration, however imperfectly.

[5]*Ibid.,* p. 112.
[6]*Ibid.,* p. 106.

If it is from the rational and efficient service of old functions that modern organizations derive their uniqueness, then it is to the society in change that we must turn for our understanding of those forces which nurture rationality and efficiency and thus hugeness in this society of organizations.

The organizational phenomenon, while far from being clearly understood, embodies at least the elements of structural, cultural, and psychological change.

The Structual Factor

The twentieth century has been characterized in the advanced states by:

1. The separation of ownership from management
2. The decline of the competitive economy and its replacement by a system of administered prices, production, and relationships between capital and labor
3. The concentration of economic power
4. The growth of science and technology
5. The development of mass production and mass markets
6. The rise in education
7. The decline of individual autonomy
8. The specialization of labor
9. The emergence of an employee society
10. The decline of the family
11. The marked increase in social mobility
12. The growth in size and power of government
13. The rise of urbanization
14. The spread of secularization
15. The startling growth in population

These sweeping changes in the societal structure, virtually occurring within the span of one lifetime, have radically modified the social controls of our society, substantially altered ideological positions, and irrevocably shifted the locus of social power. These structural alterations have encompassed the larger part of the population and have penetrated deeply into a wide range of social spheres.

The extent to which these shifts in structure has occurred is illustrated, for example, in the decline in the number of self-employed workers (nonagricultural). Between the years 1940 and 1960, in the United States, the number of these workers declined from 9,758,000 to 6,268,000, and this in spite of a considerable and continuous growth in the labor force as a whole. During the same period, the number of private wage and salary workers grew from 30 million to almost 60 million, "while government workers more than doubled, rising from 3,560,000 to 8,000,000; and in 1960 nearly half the work force, about 25,000,000, were employed by 'big organizations'."[7] More specifically, nearly one-fifth of the United States labor force in 1967 worked for the 500 largest industrial corporations whose aggregate production approximated 25 percent of the nation's total.[8]

A second illustrative measure of the scope of these changes has been the scientific revolution in industry: the chemical changes in materials; the refinements in standards and specifications; the advances in electronics, automation, and computer sciences; and the evolution in systems of energy supply. The impact of each of these revolutions within a revolution affects every level of the productive apparatus from the extraction of raw materials to final use by the ultimate consumer, the transportation and communications networks, and the intricacies of marketing, not to mention their significance for the educational system, the powers of government, and the quality of life in the broader society.[9]

A third illustrative indicator of these changes and their interrelationship may be seen in the separation of individuals from the instruments of production. If man is to work today, he must more and more be employed; for to work he must increasingly have the ever more complex and sophisticated tools and equipment which only large-scale organizations can supply. To gain access to the means of production, therefore, man becomes a worker, either blue-collar, white-collar or high-collar. As the means of production are socialized in complex organizations, man correspondingly becomes a participant in the collectivist system, less autonomous, more conformist, and increasingly dependent.

The main sociological characteristic of modernization, however, may be what Etzioni has called "differentiation," whereby rationality and efficiency are achieved and a number of specialized and distinct social units come to perform the various functions previously carried out by one social unit, the extended family. Differentiation fosters both the creation and growth of highly effective, specialized social units organized to perform the functions of production and allocation of goods, services, and wealth, and equips such units with norms and structure designed to match means and ends:

> Production, once carried out by the father and his sons, is now carried out in the factory, which is free to put younger men in charge of older ones, or group the workers in the order it finds efficient. Education is carried out by organizations in which teacher-student relations are formed according to what is considered as advancing education; they are not submerged in the elder-junior structure of the community. Even religion is largely

[7]Presthus, *op. cit.*, pp. 74 and 206.

[8]Irving Kristol, "Professor Galbraith's New Industrial State," *Fortune* (July 1967), p. 194.

[9]Robert A. Brady, *Organization, Automation, and Society* (Berkeley and Los Angeles: University of California Press, 1961), pp. 5-6.

removed from the family and tribe and invested in a structure which recruits persons whose religious leadership is more effective than that of the average father and chieftan. Allocation is not left to the primitive barter exchange, but has developed into a highly complex and organized system.[10]

This structural differentiation in turn gives rise to secondary differentiation in each of its principal spheres. Thus, the school of medicine is differentiated from the school of nursing and each in turn from the school of pharmacy; the vocational high school is differentiated from the academic high school and each as well from the reform school; the police department is differentiated from the department of social welfare, and each is further differentiated from the vice squad. Thus, rationalization and efficiency of service is extended in an ever-widening circle to encompass the diverse and variegated requirements of a heterogeneous society whose members are at once less self-sufficient and more dependent than in earlier, simpler times.

The Cultural Factor

The most extensive analysis of the place of cultural change in the organizational revolution has been made by the German sociologist, Max Weber.[11] His inquiry into the origins of large-scale economic units led him to claim that Protestantism had provided an ethos within which a rational form of organized production could rise and flourish. "Thrift, self-discipline, hard work, asceticism, worldliness—these and similar characteristics of the Protestant ethic," said Weber, "nurtured the conditions necessary for the development of capitalism, modern science, and bureaucratic organization—all three of which support one another to a large degree." If the existing social order, as the Calvinists believed, were not God's but corrupted man's doing, then man had the responsibility neither to adapt himself to his society nor to retreat into an other-worldliness. Rather, man's duty was to transform the worldly realm into the Kingdom of God. That being no small task, the cultivation of severe virtues which frowned on pleasure and smiled on disciplined living, was viewed as an essential, personal obligation for those who would join in building the Kingdom. Protestantism's two normative themes of worldliness, which requires an empirical reference and thus encourages rational behavior, and asceticism, which demands a high tolerance for frustration and discipline and, consequently, supports the rational view, combined to provide the cultural context for the organizational revolution and growth. Worldliness and asceticism, Etzioni has suggested, imply commitments not to short-term but to long-term goals: the building of a modern economy, scientific research, the devising of large-scale

---

[10]Etzioni, *op. cit.*, p. 107.

[11]Max Weber, *The Protestant Ethic and the Spirit of Capitalism,* trans. by Talcott Parsons (New York: Charles Scribner's Sons, 1958).

complex organizations—all these typify long-range tasks and a high regard for rational behavior:

> If the yields of a young economy are immediately absorbed by consumption without reinvestment, there will be no economic growth. If a scientist seeking a quick solution to a difficult problem violates the canons of empirical research, his findings will not be valid. If a bureaucrat is regularly guided by his emotions or kinship considerations rather than by established rules and procedures, the organization will be inefficient.[12]

William H. Whyte, Jr., in contrast, holds that the Protestant ethic no longer meaningfully functions in American life for her people have abandoned the hopes and ambitions which previously characterized them.[13] The ethic, he claims, rather than supporting the organizational society has today been replaced by a bureaucracy which has become the controlling end in itself. Thus, modern man looks not to his historical rootage for his security but to the big organization—corporation, government, university, military, eleemosynary, labor union, and professional association. The organization no longer derives its support and justification from the values of yesterday's ethos, says Whyte, for the bureaucracy embodies its own *raison d'être*. The large organization, J. K. Galbraith has said, is a bureaucracy first—a technostructure he calls it—and everything else last, the aim of which in the organized economic unit is security and corporate growth, in that order.[14] However, one may wish to explain cause and effect in the cultural context, the society of organizations is a present fact and demonstrably viable as it shapes and influences man in virtually every sphere of social endeavor.

The Psychological Factor

Modern organization man embraces a set of personality traits which equip him to function differentially in a loosely articulated society. In sharp contrast to primitive man whose closed society precisely stratified and defined his role and, thus, by entrapping him, ensured his security in the broader social context, contemporary man operates within a bewildering system of diverse social units that differ in their peer and authority relations, in their structure, in their goals, and in their behavioral norms. On his ability to move effectively among these various units hinges not only his own claim to income, success, and security, but the viability, rationality, and efficiency of the organizational system itself. Promptness, reliability, integrity, consistency, loyalty, neatness, and conformity

[12]Etzioni, *op. cit.,* p. 107.

[13]William H. Whyte, Jr., *The Organization Man* (Garden City, New York: Anchor Books, 1957).

[14]John Kenneth Galbraith, *The New Industrial State* (Boston: Houghton Mifflin Company, 1967).

are routinely expected attributes of organization man. But the essential characteristics include: (1) a desire to achieve; (2) an ability to postpone gratification; (3) a tolerance for frustration; (4) a willingness to compromise; and (5) a capacity and drive for disciplined work. These several qualities reflect organizational imperatives for commitment, career aspirations, functional expertise, rational behavior, and cooperation. Persons not strongly manifesting these traits are not likely to be found in the decision-making centers of complex organizations, whether large or small scale. The fact is that most functionaries in organized systems do exhibit these qualities more or less. This convergence of personality and organizational requirements broadly typifies our social environment, Etzioni believes, and is a condition owed primarily to the modern family and to the modern educational system, "both of which produce the type of person who will make a good organization man."[15] It is not the organized system, therefore, that molds men to its norms as much as it is the broader society which for whatever reason is characterized by an ethic that values highly behavioral patterns essential to organizational viability.

The Nature of Organizations

The search for more highly rational, effective and efficient organizational models has given rise to a number of competing theories of organization which fall roughly into three principal groupings: (1) the Classical School which perceives the organization as a highly structured, impersonal, and efficient instrument of social good, primarily economic and governmental, where ends are clearly delineated, means are mostly repetitive, and order is imperative. Indeed, the complex organization is seen as society's ultimate collective expression of rational action; (2) the Human Relations or Interpersonal School which views the human element as indistinguishable from the organizational imperatives for rationality and order on the assumption that individual participants in the enterprise tend "to spill over the boundaries of their segmental roles, to participate as wholes";[16] and (3) the Structuralist or Comparative School which sees the organizational phenomenon from a broader structural and cultural perspective than does either of the two other schools, and which strives to integrate the Classical and Human Relations approaches by seeing as desirable the inevitable conflict between man and the organization. This discussion of the nature of organizations will assume that formal structure and informal relationships interpenetrate and complete one another; thus, they will be considered together along with the power and authority system that integrates them.

[15]Etzioni, *op. cit.*, p. 110.

[16]Philip Selznick, "Foundations of The Theory of Organization," in Amitai Etzioni, ed., *Complex Organizations* (New York: Holt, Rinehart & Winston, Inc., 1962), pp. 26-27.

The Structure

The complex, large-scale organization is dependent for its manifest effectiveness more or less on the following general conditions:[17]

1. "Continuous organization of official functions bound by *rules.*" This imperative ensures both stable and comprehensive conditions by facilitating standardization and equality in the organization's internal relations with its clientele. This in turn reduces the power wielding elements of discretion, uncertainty, expediency, and judgment which are antithetical to organizational viability if indiscriminately and disproportionately exercised within the system.

2. "A specific sphere of competence." This ingredient of organizational life differentiates within the structure among degrees and kinds of expertise ordering these relationships systematically so that participants know not only their own boundaries of responsibility, rights, and power but, similarly, the roles of all others in the organization. Such a delineation of roles in a firmly ordered system of super- and sub-ordination markedly decreases the probability of subversion of the sort that inevitably flows from authority and responsibility in disarray.

3. "The organization of offices follows the principle of hierarchy; that is, each lower office is under the control and supervision of a higher one." As the control of the higher office over the lower implies the power to appoint, promote, and dismiss, compliance of the latter to the former is left less to chance than would otherwise be true. Thus, accountability within the system is clearly traceable both by office and by function, as bureaucratization integrates the two; and patterns of responsibility and control are more readily checked and reinforced.

4. "The rules which regulate the conduct of an office may be *technical* rules or norms. In both cases, if their application is to be fully rational, specialized training is necessary. It is thus normally true that only a person who has demonstrated an adequate technical training is qualified to be a member of the administrative staff. . . ." This principle implies that the basis of bureaucratic authority rests in the knowledge and training of the bureaucrat. Fitness for office normally involves a substantial period of formalized instruction as a condition of eligibility, measurable by examination or by similar rational procedure. Thus, it is one's attested competence that fits him for participation in the organizational society, not his social standing, his wealth, or his possession of other such traditional forms of influence.

5. "It is a matter of principle that the members of the administrative staff should be completely separated from ownership of the means of production or

[17]Max Weber, *The Theory of Social and Economic Organization,* Talcott Parsons, ed., trans. by A. M. Henderson and Talcott Parsons (New York: Oxford University Press, Inc., 1947), pp. 329-330.

administration. . . . There exists, furthermore, in principle, complete separation of the property belonging to the organization, which is controlled within the spheres of the office, and the personal property of the official. . . ." This separation, which is seen as an essential principle of organizational rationality, is not designed to prevent the official's private life from being infringed by organizational demands, but, rather, to preclude the intrusion of nonorganizational considerations on his formal bureaucratic role. To whatever extent the participant is privately influenced or monopolized by the organization's external resources, then in that measure is he constrained in the organization freely to assign organizational rationality to his bureaucratic behavior in allocating such resources.

6. "Administrative acts, decisions, and rules are formulated and recorded in writing. . . ." Only the written word within the organized setting can maintain a consistent, systematic interpretation of institutional norms and regulations. The system of control and accountability is dependent on the recorded word for its rationality and effectiveness in the same way as is the organization in its clientele relationships.

7. The remaining essential conditions necessary to organizational vitality and integrity mainly include the need to compensate by salary as against payments from clientele, to promote systematically on merit as against "influence," to reward conformity as against encouraging deviation, and to favor impersonality as against partiality.

Conditions of Survival

The basic conceptual assumption is that structure is fundamental to collective, organized rationality. Thus, maintenance of the integrity and survival of the system is the overriding imperative, to be obtained Philip Selznick suggests, by seeking:[18]

1. The security of the organization as a whole in relation to social forces in its environment
2. The stability of the lines of authority and communication
3. The stability of informal relations within the organization
4. The continuity of policy and of the sources of its determination
5. A homogeneity of outlook with respect to the meaning and role of organization

While trade unions, governments, business corporations, churches, political parties, universities, and the like are commonly conceded to be rational social units within the formal structure we have been describing, they are disparate in their ability to maintain organizational integrity and institutional survival.

[18]Selznick, *op. cit.,* pp. 26-27.

Although each strives to obtain conditions of organizational equilibrium—by institutionalizing relationships, reducing uncertainty, interchanging personnel, and manipulating the mechanisms of coordination—each perforce operates differently if it is (1) to control the conditions of its environment, and (2) to induce the participation of its members toward organizational objectives.

With respect to the first variable, the environment, S. N. Eisenstadt has suggested that the goals of the organization, the place of the goals in the societal structure, and the dependency of the organization on external forces influence greatly both its internal structure and its relation with its environment.[19]

The government bureau serves as an example. Being under less competitive pressure for survival on the environmental side, than say would be a corporate unit with marginal economic utility, the bureau, in being able largely to discount the sources of uncertainty in its environmental setting, turns its energies with undue importance to stabilizing the remaining areas of external uncertainty, to reducing internal uncertainties, and thus, to creating a stationary equilibrium which favors organizational survival. Thus, to understand the operation of a government by analyzing only the goals of the elected officials and the influence of societal demands on them is to discount the organized mechanism through which must flow whatever effective, continuous, and systematized programs the politicians desire. Indeed, as S. M. Lipset has suggested, "The goals and values of the Civil Service are at least as important a part of the total complex of forces responsible for state policy as those of the ruling political party."[20]

The second variable in organizational survival—the ability of the organization to induce the participation of its members—has captured the attention of those who see a link between human relations theories and the problem of bureaucratic dysfunctions.[21] If one believes with Michel Crozier that "human activities depend on the feelings and sentiments of the people involved, and on the interpersonal and group relationships that influence them, one cannot expect that imposing economic rationality on them will bring constant and predictable results." The functioning of a bureaucracy, therefore, "can never henceforth be totally explained by the combination of impersonality, expertness, and hierarchy of the 'ideal type.'"[22] But planned, organized, and cooperative action is possible, as has been pointed out, only if one can depend in large measure on a predictable pattern of organizational behavior on the part of its members. Or, as Crozier puts it: "any organization must obtain from its

[19]S.N. Eisenstadt, "Bureaucracy, Bureaucratization, and Debureaucratization," in Amitai Etzioni, ed., *Complex Organizations* (New York: Holt, Rinehart & Winston, Inc., 1962), p. 272.

[20]S. M. Lipset, "Bureaucracy and Social Reform," in Amitai Etzioni, ed., *Complex Organizations* (New York: Holt, Rinehart & Winston, Inc., 1962), p. 260.

[21]James March and Herbert Simon, *Organizations* (New York: John Wiley & Sons, Inc., 1958), pp. 36-47.

[22]Michel Crozier, *The Bureaucratic Phenomenon* (Chicago: University of Chicago Press, 1964), p. 179.

members a variable but always substantial amount of conformity."[23] To state the imperative, exclusively in favor of human relations, neglects the aspect of rationality and efficiency that gives the organization its *raison d'être*; and to state the imperative, exclusively in favor of the classical view, overlooks the fact that individual participants in any organized enterprise tend to function as autonomous agents out of highly personal and diverse motivations. Thus, if organizational dysfunctions relate to the delicate balance between organizational needs for order and predictive behavior, and human needs for recognition, status, autonomy, meaningful work, and personal happiness, then authority and power within the system must be so structured as to ensure conditions that will enhance the balance, not serve to advance one set of needs over that of the other.

The Authority System

In legal and political writings, the distinction between power and authority is often neglected for both refer to the ability of an individual or groups of individuals to induce others to comply. Authority and power, nevertheless, are distinguishable. Authority can be defined as the "ability to evoke compliance",[24] owing mostly to superior wisdom, expertise, prestige, or position; and power can be defined as the ability to compel adherence by coercion or force. Whereas authority relies for its use and effectiveness upon the subjects' acceptance of the values implied in its exercise—what Weber calls "legitimate power"—the use of power depends on one's capacity to impose his will on another regardless of the other's opposition. Authority and power, however, both relate to the idea of freedom in that both bear on the capacity of persons and groups of persons to make choices. How authority and power are allocated in our society and organizations is, therefore, a principal determinant the freedom individually and collectively enjoyed by the people.

The ceaseless and changing debate about the proper balance between authority, power, and freedom emerges from the efforts to organize collectively for social action; that is, when persons come together for organized purposes they are confronted with these major tasks: setting goals, differentiating functions, gathering and communicating information, assigning relationships, establishing priorities, fixing responsibility, determining rewards, allocating resources, and providing sanctions.

As reasonable people can disagree on ends as well as on means, a society collectively striving to meet its dependency-needs through organized action must make certain provision for the rational arbitration of conflicting views in ways which will not structurally or procedurally threaten, by making more dependent

[23]*Ibid.*, p. 183.
[24]Presthus, *op. cit.*, p. 195.

than the rest, any part of the enterprise. To whatever extent the dependency factor is disproportionately assigned in the society, then in that measure the system is less rational and less free, and more power than authority oriented. The place of the Negro in America is an example. The Negro does not enjoy equal participatory rights in the rational system; his rights to education, to civil rights, and to employment are generally unequal to the white man's. Thus, the Negro is more dependent for his needs on the arbitrariness of the white man than he is on the rational structure which more or less systematizes and equalizes the dependency and uncertainty factors for most of the rest of society. As he is unable, therefore, to legitimize power within the rational process, his acceptance of the system and its dictates rests less on his own willingness and more on the power of the rest of society to coerce him. The result is that he is a less free man than those who participate in the system. Men must be enabled in a rational system and a free society formally or informally to legitimize authority; otherwise, the deprived will either reject authority and the fabric of cooperative endeavor will unravel or he will behave against his will under coercion—a condition prospectively as fatal to social order and cohesiveness as is anarchy.

Modern institutional order in the developed state is characterized by what Weber has called "rational-legal authority" by which he means bureaucratic authority or the authority of the impersonal order itself which grants legitimate power to individuals according to their office under written rules—authority which is exercisable only within the bureaucratic structure and only so long as the individual occupies the office. Within Weber's bureaucracy, men hold their positions by virtue of their fitness to perform the task. Thus, their power is legitimized for it reflects both expertise and position within a system impersonally ordered to maximize rational decision-making and to minimize arbitrary and illogical actions. While rational-legal authority is less stable than "traditional" authority—authority reliant on kinships, inherited rights, and status which was commonly found in medieval society—it is more stable than "charismatic authority" which depends for its effectiveness and legitimation on discipleships, moral precept, and the personal magnetism of leaders during times of severe social disorder and widespread uncertainty as in Nazi Germany in 1933, Bolshevik Russia in 1917, and revolutionary France in 1789. The rigidity of traditional authority and the unpredictability of charismatic authority are in a complex society equally unacceptable means of rationally coming to terms with the perplexing and volatile demands of modern civilization. Indeed, the predominance not of these two forms of authority but of rational-legal authority in the advanced industrial states is central to them and to whatever liberties their peoples enjoy.

While the development of rational-legal authority with bureaucratic administration has been both dependent on the breakdown of traditional authority and on the containment of charismatic authority, it has not resulted in a monolithic-authority network characterized by centralized decision-making. Rather, the result has been a highly complicated, structured decentralization of the organizational process into pluralistic semiautonomous subsystems. This network of delicately interacting and interconnected parts reflects the diversity of views about means and ends that only free men will overtly exhibit, the tolerance for change that so typifies our culture, and the unwillingness to generalize any single solution, as Crozier points out:

> The greater confidence effected by the progress of knowledge, the possibilities of mastering the environment that is implies, have not tended to reinforce the rigidity of the decision-making process. They seem, on the contrary, to have obliged organizations to discard completely the very notion of *one best way.* The most advanced organizations, because they now feel capable of integrating areas of uncertainty in their economic calculus, are beginning to understand that the illusion of perfect rationality has too long persisted, weakening the possibilities of action by insisting on rigorous logic and immediate coherence. Substituting the notion of program for the notion of operational process, introducing the theory of probability at lower and lower levels, reasoning on global systems, and integrating more and more variables without separating ends and means, they are experiencing a deep and irreversible change. The crucial point of this change consists, for us, in recognizing—first implicitly, then more and more consciously—that man cannot look for the one best way and has not actually even searched for it. The philosophy of the one best way has been only a way of protecting oneself against the difficulty of having to choose, a scientist's substitute for the traditional ideologies upon which rested the legitimacy of the rulers' decisions. Man has never been able to search for the *optimum* solution. He has always had to be content with solutions merely *satisfactory* in regard to a few particularistic criteria of which he was aware.[25]

Centralized authority is further mitigated by the following two factors: (1) the separation-of-powers concept; as the separation in governmental structure between legislative, executive, and judicial authority; and (2) to the presence of collegial bodies of equals in the place of hierarchy; as in the authority of expertise embodied in the university faculty. These two factors and the forces discussed by Crozier produce wide variations in organizational structure and process. The corporate unit organized to produce goods will serve to illustrate the point. However large, complex, and decentralized it may be, this organizational model, especially in its manufacturing processes, will tend to favor hierarchial authority in the classical style. The uncertainties of the market, the predictable pressures of labor, and the complexity of inducing participation from vast numbers of skilled, semiskilled, and unskilled workers all press toward

[25]Crozier, *op. cit.,* p. 159.

the organizational imperatives of more rather than less control of subordinates by superior offices, tighter rather than looser structure, impersonal rather than partial human relations, and a low rather than a high tolerance for individual discretion. A university, on the other hand, with relatively few skilled or semiskilled workers and large numbers of highly trained professional persons engaged autonomously in a bewildering array of diverse endeavors at levels of sophistication understood only by peers clearly demands a looser rather than a tighter structure, less rather than more hierarchy, high rather than low tolerance for individual judgment and discretion, and a wide rather than a narrow band of delegated administrative authority to coordinate with the authority of expertise collectively present in the body of scholars.

Organizational Dysfunction

What is conspicuous, however, about the modern organizational society is not so much the complexity and variety of its organized forms, but that they are nearly all variations on the same theme; that is, they are rational, effective, and efficient units characterized by hierarchy, differentiation of function, impersonality, and order, and integrated by the Weberian concept of rational-legal authority—however centralized or decentralized the unit may be, however hierarchical or diffused authority may be, however useful or esoteric organizational ends may be, or however large or small the scale of operation may be. Robert Presthus has observed that "artistic, educational, and spiritual activities have embraced bureaucratic organization, seeking efficiency, and confusing size with grandeur as fully as their industrial counterparts. In adopting the techniques of commerce," Presthus continues, "they have inevitably adopted some of its values, and their character has changed accordingly."[26] Indeed, for modern man, the omnipresent organization constitutes the arena, the mechanism whereby man wins or loses success, power, and personal worth. In terms of quality and of human values, however, the effect of large-scale organized endeavor "on art, liberal education, and mass communication is," for Presthus and others, "a disturbing question."[27]

Impact on Higher Education

Consider for a moment the impact of this condition of hugeness and impersonality on education at the higher levels. In September of 1964, Bradford Cleaveland wrote the following which was widely distributed on the Berkeley campus of the University of California when the Free Speech Movement was in its nascent state:

[26]Presthus, *op. cit.*, p. 20.
[27]*Ibid.*

The salient characteristic of the multiversity is massive production of specialized excellence. The multiversity is actually not an educational center but a highly efficient industry engaged in producing skilled individuals to meet the immediate needs of business or government. . . .

Below the level of formal power and responsibility (the Regents, president and chancellors), the faculty itself is guilty of a massive and disastrous default. More concerned with their own increasingly affluent specialized careers, they have permitted an administrative process to displace, and become an obstruction to, extended thought and learning for the undergraduate. Professors have made a gift of the undergraduate learning situation to the bureaucrat. . . .

The process [of education] is a four-year-long series of sharp staccatos: eight semesters, forty courses, one hundred twenty or more "units," ten to fifteen impersonal lectures *per week,* and one to three oversized discussion meetings per week led by poorly paid unlearned graduate students.[28]

"Do not bend, fold, or mutilate," read the IBM cards pinned to the front of those students at Berkeley who regarded their University not as a center of learning but as an "impersonal bureaucracy," a "machine," and "knowledge factory." Education, they claimed, had been usurped and demeaned in favor of bureaucracy; that is, in preference to having learning as its end the University had chosen instead to produce men for the organizational society whose values and competencies would mesh with the needs of government and industry. Thus, it was asserted, the University typified in its structure and processes the same characteristics as would be found in other organized efforts calculated to produce measured and standardized goods and services. The University's bureaucracy had placed a premium on precision, efficiency, speed, control, continuity and similar administrative measures which optimized returns on input, depersonalized human relationships, and minimized nonrational considerations. Not only that, these students argued, but the rigid enforcement of rules designed not so much to enhance the learning process as to facilitate the administrative process had displaced the goals of education by becoming themselves the terminal values of organizational effort. Set against the learning ideals of free inquiry and expression, personal worth, spontaneity, and individual autonomy, the organizational claims, at least for these students, were dysfunctional. Indeed, personal freedom and progress, measured by these students in terms of effective choices and meaningful participation in the educational process, had for them been subverted by what they regarded as centralized power and decision-making. The acquisitive demands of our society had, as they understood it, subordinated the University's real values and

[28]Bradford Cleaveland, "Education, Revolutions, and Citadels," in A. M. Lipset and S. S. Wolin, eds., *The Berkeley Student Revolt* (New York: Anchor Books, 1965), pp. 89-90.

aspirations. The University in turn and inevitably had regarded them as instruments rather than as ends.

The implications of a university subverted by the dysfunctions of bureaucracy carry significant meaning for the faculty as well as for the students. Citing evidence of the extent to which organizational expectations and rewards influence individual behavior, Presthus has commented on the power struggles and professional commitments which typify departmental life in the modern university:

> The underlying reason [for the dysfunction] is the passionate specialization of the university organization. All the dynamics of training, of values, and of professional recognition push one toward restricted fields of analysis. As a result, trained incapacity, technical introversion, and bureaucratic infighting are characteristic of most university departments.[29]

Moreover, dysfunction occurs when those most qualified to make rational judgments are structured out of the decision-making process as is often true in contemporary university and college administration. Structure and process in higher learning today find the professional increasingly alientated, the administration aggrandized, and ultimate power vested in laymen whose values often run counter to those collectively held by the faculty and students and whose competence to make educational decision is clearly peripheral.[30]

The Culture as a Constraint

The university condition illustrates in microcosm the quite unwanted dysfunctions of bureaucracy which generally, although in quite different fashion, typify the stresses which arise when organizational imperatives for order, efficiency, rationality, and impersonality confront human needs for autonomy, personal worth, and spontaneity. The example also points up the fact that organizations are not merely contrivances to provide goods and services, but constitute the environment in which most of us spend most of our lives:

> In their efforts to rationalize human energy they become sensitive and versatile agencies for the control of man's behavior, employing subtle psychological sanctions that evoke desired responses and inculcate consistent patterns of action. In this sense, big organizations are a major disciplinary force in our society. Their influence spills over the boundaries of economic interest or activity into spiritual and intellectual sectors; the

---

[29]Presthus, *op. cit.*, p. 12.

[30]For an in depth study of these forces at work in a major university during times of crises, see David P. Gardner, *The California Oath Controversy* (Berkeley and Los Angeles: University of California Press, 1967).

accepted values of the organization shape the individual's personality and influence his behavior in extravocational ways.[31]

Thus, large-scale organizations socialize their values through their authority and reward system, their unrivaled capacity to manipulate, and their centrality in modern man's pattern of survival. Culture, on the other hand, does act as a constraint on organizational character. Those societies, for example, which place great stress on authoritarian models, little emphasis on education for the masses, and considerable value on strict order in the home and school experience are most likely to emerge with an organizational pattern which favors a hierarchial bureaucracy in the rigid, classical sense; whereas, those societies which value equality of social relationships, mass education, and permissiveness in the home and school environment are more likely to develop a loosely articulated, pluralistic, highly diffused organizational situation. Complex organizations in Germany reflect German culture,[32] as those in Britain are permeated by the British culture,[33] and as those in Japan bear the stamp of Japanese culture.[34] The American organizational pattern, as with the examples above, is stamped with the character of the culture which nurtures it and is more than not typified by the deep-seated sentiments in our society which oppose the use of men as instruments of impersonal ends (shocking exceptions include, among others, the use of Negro slaves in the agricultural south, the employment of Chinese in the building of the western railroads, and the use of child labor and women in the sweat shops which accompanied our earlier industrialization). The cultural bias which places a high valuation on individual worth has caused men to impede, through the enactment of antitrust legislation, the encouragement of unionism and the establishment of regulatory agencies, the otherwise dominant trend toward central authority and economic monopoly. Of course, the system remains imperfect as inevitably it must in any volatile, dynamic, and shifting social scene. Moreover, organizations while existing with the consent of the surrounding society do not automatically fall under societal control. But however one may view the contributions of the organization to and its dysfunctions in American life we are for better or for worse an organizational society:

We are born in organizations, educated by organizations, and most of us spend much of our lives working for organizations. We spend much of our

[31]Presthus, *op. cit.*, p. 16.

[32]Heinz Hartmann, *Authority and Organization in German Management* (Princeton, N.J.: Princeton University Press, 1959).

[33]Stephen A. Richardson, "Organizational Contrasts on British and American Ships," *Administrative Science Quarterly,* Vol. 1 (September 1956), pp. 189-207.

[34]James C. Abegglen, *The Japanese Factory,* (New York: Free Press of Glencoe, Inc., 1958).

leisure time paying, playing, and praying in organizations. Most of us will die in an organization and when the time comes for burial, the largest organization of all—the state—must grant official permission.[35]

Summary

Modern organizations have made collective, rational, and effective action possible in a time characterized by large scale human endeavor. Their predominance is not incidental, but central to the development of Western civilization. The principal social mechanism for translating ideas into viable, workable programs and for arbitrating the myriad wants of man is the organization; and we are reliant on it for the maintenance and enhancement of our most cherished freedoms and most important liberties. Our chances for security, position, success, and happiness are inseparable from it. Whether we shall be masters or servants of our collective selves will depend on our ability to cope with the vital dysfunctions of the system, especially as they affect the integrity of the individual human being.

Annotated Bibliography

Argyris, C., *Interpersonal Competence and Organizational Effectiveness.* Dorsey Press, Homewood, Ill., 1962. This book, which relies mostly on industrial data, combines psychoanalytical with administrative perspectives.

Brady, R. A., *Organization, Automation, and Society* University of California Press, Berkeley, 1961. This work attempts to answer how society can best organize its productive resources to make full use of the scientific and technological revolution.

Bryson, L., Finkelstein, L., Maciver, R., and McKeon, R. (eds.), *Freedom and Authority in Our Time.* Harper & Row, Publishers, New York, 1953. This volume includes the papers presented at the Twelfth meeting of the Conference of Science, Philosophy, and Religion. The essays deal with freedom and authority in virtually every aspect of democratic life: governmental, legal, cultural, moral, religious, individual, academic, and so forth.

Cleveland, H., and Lasswell, H. (eds.), *Ethics and Bigness: Scientific, Academic, Religious, Political, and Military.* Harper & Row, Publishers, New York, 1962. This volume includes the papers presented at the Sixteenth meeting of the

[35]Etzioni, *op. cit.,* p. 1.

Conference on Science, Philosophy and Religion. These papers are concerned with the problems of size and morals in large-scale organizations.

Crozier, Michel, *The Bureaucratic Phenomenon.* University of Chicago Press, Chicago, 1964. This book, by a French author, draws together the experience of France and the United States with organizational systems and reports extensively from field investigations concerned with monopoly, power, structure, and personality.

Dalton, M., *Men Who Manage.* John Wiley & Sons, Inc., New York, 1959. This work is a sociological study of executives functioning in the organizational system, largely descriptive in its approach.

Etzioni, Amitai (ed.), *Complex Organizations.* Holt, Rinehart & Winston, Inc., New York, 1962. This book is a selection of mostly recent contributions to the study of structure, goals, and environment of the organized social unit.

Etzioni, Amitai, *Modern Organizations.* Prentice-Hall, Inc., Englewood Cliffs, N.J., 1964. This small book deals with the organization in modern society in terms of structure, control, and authority systems and in relation to the member, the client, and the social environment.

Gardner, David P., *The California Oath Controversy.* University of California Press, Berkeley, 1967. This work reports the controversy of 1949-52 that raged in the University of California over a loyalty oath required of the faculty by The Regents and the organizational dysfunctions which attended that dispute.

Lipset, S. M., and Wolin, S. S. (eds.), *The Berkeley Student Revolt.* Anchor Books, New York, 1965. This book is a collection of essays concerned with the Berkeley Free Speech Movement of 1964-65, many of them authored by the major figures in that protest movement, and most of them dealing with the principal issues of that controversy.

March, J., and Simon, H., *Organizations.* John Wiley & Sons, Inc., New York, 1958. This work is concerned with the theory of the formal organization and deals with organizational behavior, motivation, conflict, planning, innovation, and rationality.

Presthus, Robert, *The Organizational Society.* Alfred A. Knopf, Inc., New York, 1962. This book is an interdisciplinary analysis of big complex organizations and the influence of them on their members and on the broader society.

Selznick, P., *Leadership in Administration.* Harper & Row, Publishers, New York, 1957. This essay studies leadership in administrative organizations from a more reflective and theoretical perspective than do most works.

Stroup, Herbert, *Bureaucracy in Higher Education.* Free Press of Glencoe, Inc., New York, 1966. This book will be of interest to students of higher education who wish to review that phenomenon from the perspective of structure and function in the bureaucratic state.

Thompson, James D., *Organizations in Action,* McGraw-Hill Book Company, New York, 1967. This work is a conceptual inventory of organization theory which focuses on the behavior of organizations.

CHAPTER 6

The Mass Media and Politics

J. Herschel Parsons

J. Herschel Parsons is Managing Editor of the Glendessary Press, academic publishers of social science materials. She is co-author with sociologist Donald A. Hansen of Mass Communication: A Research Bibliography.

Introduction

To date the study of the mass media has remained the concern of professional sociologists and journalists with little information reaching the teacher in training, much less the secondary student. The study of structure and content has been left to a superficial level of consideration in secondary English and journalism classes, with functional implications largely ignored in the social studies classes beyond mention of World War II propaganda techniques and the persuasion potential of advertising. When the propaganda issue is raised, teachers warn to students to beware of its possible effects and illustrate the case with examples of Hitler's successes. The student gets the message but somewhere in his mind he probably remembers that Hitler is, after all, dead, and, furthermore, Vietnam is not a world war and therefore does not warrant such serious consideration. Discussions of the subtle distortions that might occur between an event and the reporting of that event are seldom considered, and the student is not exposed to the differing processes and structures that contribute to the interpretations of a message once it is received. Political and socio-cultural considerations are lost, usually in a shuffle of priorities, with considerations of the media reaching perhaps a third or fourth level of importance following the "more immediate" concerns of government, public opinion, voting, and other standard curriculum study areas. This is not to minimize the importance of these subjects but rather to call attention to the lack of concern for the *equally* important political implications of the mass media as an entity in itself. Exclusion of the processes and effects of the mass media of communications contributes to the already existing "wasteland" of knowledge about emerging processes that occupy an increasing number of the waking hours in the life of nearly every individual in this complex society.

The purpose of this chapter, then, is to acquaint the teacher with some aspects of mass communication study that could be used as a focus in the classroom. The emphasis on "news" has been chosen for its immediate relation to the political and social processes that are generally the concern of social studies curriculum. A brief background of some concerns in mass communication research will be presented, followed by a review of some of the material currently found in textbooks. Some problems of the media used in political processes will then be explored along with a consideration of what constitutes news. The large part of the chapter will deal with those problem areas that can be used as possible classroom topics.

Background

Mass communication research has been developing since the 1920's when the rapid growth of the media began to encourage large audiences. With the advent of World War II, psychologists and sociologists became systematically interested in the subject area and designed sophisticated research projects that produced a number of findings focusing on the area of propaganda. As the media continued to grow in number, advertising effects held the attention of researchers interested in persuasive communications. An apparent nagging motive behind this search for audience reactions was the threat of the development of a "mass society."

The concept of the "mass" developed with the increase in urbanization and the decrease in primary group associations. A mass society can be simply described as society in which the members are spatially separated and not necessarily known to each other; these are heterogeneous individuals who do not constitute any one group with common customs, traditions, or rules governing their behavior. These individuals may be easily mobilized or stirred to action, for their lack of mediating restraints make them highly vulnerable to suggestion; thus the mass media, which can potentially be a means for reaching and possibly mobilizing these people, become an important concern.

Research findings have subsequently discouraged the myth of a direct flow of communication from communicator to receiver. Individuals, it has been found, do not necessarily receive messages as they are sent but rather a built-in filtering system, based on previous experiences, selects and interprets each message received. This pattern can better be described as a multi-step process in which messages are both filtered and modified.

This process is facilitated if the individual is committed to multiple and diverse autonomous groups. These groups, with their differing norms and values, mediate between the communicator's message and the receiver to allow discrimination and distillation of the ideas received. This is one ingredient of a pluralistic, democratic system.[1]

A "classic" democratic model is based on the premise that truth and justice will emerge from free discussion. The process can be simplistically described as follows:

> . . .an issue arises that is salient enough for people's concern, they gather in small groups to discuss the issue, decisions are made that form a "point of view," this is compared and debated with divergent "points of view" from other groups, open discussion allows the formulation of a synthesis which becomes a "public opinion," this is presented to the representative government to be formalized into law.[2]

In order to initiate the process of public opinion formation, individuals must be in touch with the "facts" of the issue. Members of contemporary society are now in possession of the means for disseminating these facts, but a closer view of the process of mass communication raises questions as to how faithfully the agencies of this process are fulfilling the traditional role. This role of the press (which includes all newsgathering agencies) has been that of a mediator between the government and the individual; more specifically as a "watchdog" on the government. It appears, however, that this process is being perverted. What effect has increased governmental control of news had on this process? What other subtler processes are in effect that additionally control and manage the news, thereby restricting free discussion? These, and others, are problems that can and should be discussed in the social studies classroom. The student should be exposed to these present day problems if he is to effectively interpret news received from the media, generally his only link with events beyond his immediate environment.

What Is Offered in the Classroom

The assumption has been made here that the textbook forms the basic source material for a social studies class; it is the structural support of the subject matter with which the teacher works. That is, if a subject is ignored or inadequately presented in the text it is not likely that it will be studied with

---

[1] For an extensive discussion of the elements of a pluralistic, totalitarian or mass society, see William Kornhauser, *The Politics of a Mass Society* (New York: Free Press of Glencoe, Inc., 1959).

[2] C. Wright Mills, "Mass Media and Public Opinion," *Power, Politics and People* (New York: Ballantine Books, Inc., 1939), pp. 577-598.

much depth in the classroom.[3] With this assumption, a sample of the current social studies textbooks was studied for inclusion of information on the subject of mass communications. The books chosen were primarily those which dealt with discussions of the polity or social problems; history books were not included. Sample results shown in the addendum, indicate a general lack of concern for the political and socio-cultural implications of the mass media. The number of pages found concerning the subject were often cumulative, gathering scattered bits of information from various sections. A rating of a book as "poor" or "good" was the writer's subjective evaluation and not based on any "measurable" criterion; it referred only to the handling of the subject under discussion and in no way was a reflection of the other subject matter presented.

The most frequently mentioned aspect of mass communications was the control measures used by the Federal Communications Commission, including discussions that highly exaggerated the actual amount of influence that agency has exerted over program content. Second in popularity was discussions of propaganda techniques which were brief in coverage and biased in presentation. The more conscientious handlings included a discussion of what is desirable in a source, listing ideal criteria for selection and use. Aside from the fact that these criteria tended to be highly biased in selection, there was little account given to the fact that many students will, in their adult life, seldom read more than headlines, let alone expose themselves to any of the few "prestige press." Through the intention of these discussions is to expose the student to the more reliable of news sources, the effort might have been expanded to a discussion of why it is advantageous to choose one of these sources and in what way the less desirable sources fall short of the "ideal."

The text, supplemented by teacher's instruction should strive to develop an understanding of the complexities involved in the news gathering and disseminating agencies, exposing him to the subtle but existing biases that are often present. A fuller understanding may possibly have the more latent effect of reducing the high degree of an individual's alienation from political involvement that exists in the population by broadening his levels of awareness of the processes operating in his environment. The news is for the individual a link to the community at large. The teacher can help him *interpret* information received about this extended environment, transforming the "informed" individual into an "insightful" one.

Selected Problems Faced by the Media

The news media can be generally divided into newspapers, magazines, television, and radio, each having fairly unique means of communicating

[3] C. Benjamin Cox and Byron G. Massialas, eds., make a similar case for the importance of the textbook in the determination of the subject matter taught in *Social Studies in the United States: A Critical Appraisal* (New York: Harcourt, Brace & World, Inc., 1967), p. 7.

information and consequently, appealing to slightly different audiences. The print media tend to appeal to the more informed and educated individual who seeks news in more detail than those who attend solely to an electronic medium which is used more for entertainment. The print media are differentiated by their focus of presentation, newspapers relate only news of the day while magazines tend to analyze and discuss broader issues to a greater extent. The visual character of television readily distinguishes its approach from radio which is purely audio. The following comments and study descriptions help to demonstrate the differing perspectives and influences that are operant.

Newspapers

Newspapers are produced and distributed within regional boundaries and are directed toward all strata of that geographic area. This medium becomes vulnerable to certain local values or prejudices which cause some degree of cross-pressure between local influences when they oppose national values or codes of press "responsibility." This is exemplified in a study by Charles Higbie, who conducted a content analysis of a random sample of ninety United States newspapers on the coverage of book reviews on subjects related to civil rights. He found that books on racial discrimination fared less well in the South than in the North. Fewer readers in the South have the opportunity to be exposed to such books, and when reviews did appear they received slightly less favorable treatment than those in the Northern papers. The race of the author showed no appreciable difference between the two areas.[4] Thus, some papers appear to avoid the problem of cross-value pressures by not approaching the subject while others succumb to the local traditions.

Magazines

The political magazine serves to meet the needs of the reader who wishes an in-depth discussion of news events. Though readers have come to recognize editorial "bias" in each one, and generally attend to the one that most closely approximates their specific *Weltanschauung,* editorializing can be so cleverly subtle that it is sometimes mistaken for "straight reporting." For example, John Merrill found that *Time* magazine editorialized in its regular news columns to a great extent by employing a variety of "tricks" to bias its stories and "lead" the reader's thinking. This was done primarily in its treatment of Presidential news. The study, covering the terms of three presidents, found that *Time* was clearly anti-Truman, strongly pro-Eisenhower and neutral or moderate toward Kennedy. This effect was achieved by a stereotyping of images through a type of "subjectivizing procedures." Merrill found such devices as the differential

[4] Charles E. Higbie, "Book Reviewing and Civil Rights: The Effect of Regional Opinion," *Journalism Quarterly,* vol. 41 (1964), pp. 385-394.

handling of reportorial quotations: "Truman said curtly," or "with his voice heavy with sarcasm"; "Eisenhower said with a happy grin," or "skillfully refused to commit himself"; "Kennedy announced," or "stated the case in plain terms."[5]

The psychological effect here is fairly evident: by introducing the suggestion of positive or negative affect prior to a quotation, it is assumed to be part of the *fact* or *unbiased* report, whereas it actually amounts to a heavily weighted but subtly presented suggestion of acceptance or rejection of the quotation itself.

Television

Television has the largest audience of the mass media, catering to the most diverse of the population who attend for the greatest number of hours. This medium has recently undergone a great deal of criticism for its leanings toward program choice based on a "lowest common denominator" criterion. Its bland presentation is a guarantee not to offend any group of people who are large enough in number or powerful enough in status to apply the pressure of censorship.

Television, importantly, presents a unique perspective when viewing the reporting of events. This is due to the nature of presentation which is both audio and visual; the individual assumes a false reality of being an "eyewitness" to the event viewed. Kurt and Gladys Lang conducted a study of the MacArthur Day parade in Chicago, following the General's release of command in the Far East in 1951. They made a content analysis of (1) the selections made by the camera and their structuring of the event in terms of foreground and background, and (2) the explanations and interpretations of the televised events given by commentators and persons interviewed by them. These were compared with eyewitness accounts of trained observers at the event. They found a great discrepancy in the two perspectives. The television camera had the advantage of choosing the picture to be presented with a close-up and then moving on to another focus. The only excitement that occurred in the crowd was when MacArthur was actually on the spot, but those viewing the scene on television followed the moving camera which gave the distorted picture of the entire crowd being in a constant state of excitement. The process of televising the event added to the excitement when the camera was focused on a group of people; what many people at home were witnessing was actually the crowd's enthusiasm of being filmed rather than the excitement of seeing MacArthur. The effect of this distorted picture on the home screen was the false image of overwhelming public

[5] John C. Merrill, "How *Time* Stereotyped Three U.S. Presidents," *Journalism Quarterly,* vol. 42 (1965), pp. 563-570.

sentiment in favor of the General, creating a disposition for increased support or a "land-slide" effect.[6]

Radio

Many people today use a great number of the hours previously spent listening to radio for the viewing of television. Formerly, audiences expected various satisfactions from the radio, entertainment ranging from their favorite fictional programs to in-depth coverage of the news of the day. These functions have been taken over, for the most part, by the television screen. Still, there are a great number of radios distributed among the population, and many people continue to spend many hours listening to them.

Harold Mendelson made a study of the AM radio audience of New York City in 1961 to discover the variety of radio functions beyond the obvious provisions of entertainment and news. He found that (1) a basic *mood function* exists—"that of sustaining and creating desired psychological climates"; (2) radio serves a *companionship function* filling the voids created by daily tedious work and feelings of loneliness; (3) a large percentage of those interviewed depended on radio a "great deal" for its *utilitarian and news function* and that they would seldom switch off a given station's news broadcast even though they had chosen that station to listen to music and had already heard the news; and (4) radio serves a *social function*—it is a "social lubricant" by providing listeners with things to talk about; for example, the housewife who is home all day with only the children and the housework listens to radio so that she can discuss the day's happenings with her husband when he returns home.

He also found that listeners do not expect one station to fulfill all roles and people will switch from one station to another to meet their shifting needs.[7] He concluded that the major functions of radio can be said to be (1) utilitarian information and news (2) active mood accompaniment (3) release from psychological tension and pressure and (4) friendly companionship.

What Is News?

The answer to the question, "What is news?" is not as easily resolved as one might suppose. It could, perhaps, be simplistically defined as, "knowledge about an event"; but how much knowledge, and how closely must this knowledge adhere to the reality of the event? Is rumor news? Tomatsu Shibutani suggests:

---

[6] Kurt and Gladys Lang, "The Unique Perspective of Television," *American Sociological Review*, vol. 18 (1953), pp. 3-12.

[7] Harold Mendelson, "Listening to Radio," in Lewis A. Dexter and David M. White, eds., *People, Society and Mass Communications* (New York: Free Press of Glencoe, Inc., 1964), pp. 239-249.

Since news has immediate relevance to action that is already under way, it is perishable. This suggests that news is not merely something new; it is information that is timely. Even if it is about events long past, the information is necessary for current adjustment; it relieves tension in the immediate situation. For this reason news has an ephemeral career.... When nothing more can be done about events recorded in a newspaper, those items also cease to be news. This transient quality is the very essence of news, for an event ceases to be newsworthy as soon as the tension it has aroused has been dissipated. Once a decision has been reached, the quickening sense of urgency and importance disappears, and public attention turns elsewhere.[8]

A concern for immediately receiving reports of events has become a near mania in the electronic age of communication. There is the old cliché, "there's nothing as old as yesterday's news," and a new phrase, coined by a radio station, "when you hear it, it's news, when you read it, it's history." News must be a "happening" to receive attention. This presentation of the news, of course, is only a mention of the existence of an event; there are no details and no discussion. The implication is that it is more important to have *heard* of the event than to *know about* it in any detail.

Pressures of time and priority compound problems in the flow of news from the source to the audience. The many "gates" that the report must pass through before coming to rest as history create a risk of distortion or elimination. Walter Gieber concludes:

The flow of information in the extended newsgathering channels containing multiple communicators is a complex in which each gate area is in a separate frame of reference and in which each gate area contains a bureaucratic structure. The ultimate additors — the mass-media audience — serve as a dimly perceived, generalized frame of reference overlying specific reference clusters. One may conclude that all news is fragile.[9]

News describes events that are violations of "expected" behavior—behavior that is in keeping with the dominant social and political norms. Occurrences of deviance make sensational news and are presented in specific contexts. That is, deviance is generally presented as a unique example and there is little transference to the general case. Simple causation is often assigned; it is easier to present, and accept a scapegoat (for example, a riot is presented as being a single agitator or specific group of agitators) than to investigate the more complex problem of poverty or suppression.

[8]Tamotsu Shibutani, *Improvised News: A Sociological Study of Rumor* (Indianapolis, Ind.: The Bobbs-Merrill Co., Inc., 1967), p. 41.
[9]Walter Gieber, "Two Communicators of the News: A Study of the Roles of Sources and Reporters," *Social Forces,* vol. 39 (1960), p. 83.

Related to this idea is the fact that certain individuals and groups are able to remain "out of the public's eye." This is accomplished, in great part, by the selection that occurs in the newsroom. Warren Breed has found that the media maintain socio-cultural consensus by the omission of certain items by burying those which jeopardize the existing structure and man's faith in it. He did a "reverse content check" of more than 250 items that clustered around central institutional areas. He found:

> . . .by far the most frequent finding focused around the politico-economic area, or more specifically, what we might call "the undemocratic power of business elites." Roughly two-thirds of the items presumably "buried" by the press were of this type. Religion ranked second, with about one-fifth of the total. The remaining notes were concerned with such areas as justice, health, and the family.[10]

He also found that certain types of individuals received favorable treatment such as doctors, business leaders, judges, mothers, clergymen, and G.I.'s overseas. He concludes that this leads to the proposition that "leaders personify or embody the values related to their office." Therefore, by avoiding criticism of these representative individuals, the media, by omission, are supporting the organizations that they represent and therefore are also supporting the status quo — the existing cultural values.

News, it seems, must be considered as a dynamic phenomenon; a "process" in which much selection and omission occurs due to various perception and pressures. This concept has been explored by Donald A. Hansen in his lectures on a sociology of the news. He describes this perspective:

> A sociology of the news, that is, might attend the "news" (as a structural component) as but one aspect of the "news process," of a continuing activity involving both formal and informal channels which interlink individuals both in structured organizational positions and in informal interpersonal relationships. . . . One part of this process is the news report: From the on-going activity of these individuals and organizations, artifacts — formal messages — at times distill, and some, but not all, of these messages are "news." For example, to focus on but one of the many relationships in the process: reporter and source are linked in communication channels which may be continuing or transient, well-defined or ambiguous. In these channels, involving interchanges in both directions, the reporter gains information necessary for his story — that is, necessary for the distillation and transmission over the formal channel to the news agency. On acceptance by the agency, this artifact

---

[10]Warren Breed, "Mass Communication and Socio-Cultural Integration," *Social Forces,* vol. 37 (1958), p. 111.

undergoes further modification, not only as a result of the personal make-up of the "gatekeepers," but also of the organizational constraints, the relationships of the agency of reporter, to source, to formal and informal organizations within the community, and to the receiving news organization, and of the established channels over which the modified messages must be transmitted.

That is, the news process and, more generally, mass communication, involves both formal and informal channels (both transient and continuing) linking individuals and organizations (both informal and formal); intermittently form these process relationships are distilled formal statements, some of which (after varied modifications and further distillations) appear as formally presented news reports. This statement . . . should not be read to imply that the news process is linear, originating in the source and ending in the nonreader; rather, it is a systemic process in which activity in any part of the system might stimulate changes in other parts.[11]

News is not always used solely to report a spontaneous event, but is also used as a means of heightening and maintaining a degree of attention: that is, the sustaining of tensions as described by Shibutani, or the creation of interest through appeal to the emotions, such as the "human interest story," or the more widely disdained "yellow journalism." Other forms of news can be said to be initiated primarily for the sake of having an event to report; this type of news will now be discussed.

The Formation of News

The Pseudo-Event

Technological advances have created an opportunity for round-the-clock news. As events are not always conveniently arranged in this manner, it often becomes necessary for news "gathering" to turn into news "making." That is, events reported throughout a day are not all reports of spontaneous events, but, rather, many are *created,* oftentimes merely for the sake of having some news to report. The characteristics that Daniel Boorstin suggests to describe this type of news are: (1) it is not spontaneous but has occurred because someone has planned it; (2) it is planned primarily for the immediate purpose of being reported; (3) the relation to underlying reality of the situation is ambiguous; and

[11]Donald A. Hansen, lecture notes, University of California, Santa Barbara, 1966.

(4) it is usually intended to be a self-fulfilling prophecy. An event of this type is referred to as a "pseudo-event."[12]

An accomplished master of the pseudo-event was the late Senator Joseph R. McCarthy of Wisconsin, who created news with each vague accusation of "creeping communism." He began his campaign early in 1950 by presenting a flood of defenseless accusations which, once it had washed over his victim, left the person struggling for social survival. As stated by Richard Rovere: "Senator Charges Communist Influence in State Department" might have produced a two-inch story on page fifteen of the local newspaper. "Over Two Hundred with Communist Ties" would have done slightly better. But "Two Hundred and Fifty" card carrying communists was something else. It was as if the press yearned for the really big lie."[13] Newsmen were hungry for his proclamations even when they disapproved of both his techniques and purposes.

A less sensational but more recent pseudo-event of large scale was the Great Debate series between John F. Kennedy and Richard Nixon prior to the 1960 presidential election. It became apparent that far more interest was shown in the performance than in what was said. It finally became an "issue" as to whether there should be a fifth debate; an example of one pseudo-event creating another.[14]

The pseudo-event has great appeal beyond the immediate need as a time filler. Boorstin suggests that they can be (1) more dramatic; (2) planned for easier dissemination; (3) reported at will and reinforced; (4) when appropriate, advertised in advance; (5) more intelligible; (6) more sociable, conversable and convenient to witness; (7) an index of being "informed"; and (8) a spawner of other pseudo-events in geometric progression – as in the case of the Great Debates.[15]

It is important that students be able to distinguish between "spontaneous" and "pseudo" events to be better able to interpret news and maintain a proper balance of the knowledge they seek and receive from the media. Some topics that can be discussed in the classroom will be considered in the following pages. Spontaneous events, such as natural calamities, or reports of accidents and crime will not be covered, though the differential handling of these types of news, too, is well worth studying in the classroom. The concern here will be the more obvious cases of "prepared" news to illustrate some subject areas that can be approached

---

[12]Daniel Boorstin, "From News Gathering to News Making: A Flood of Pseudo-Events," *The Image*, (Baltimore, Md.: Penguin Books, Inc., 1961), pp. 19-54.

[13]Douglas Cater, *The Fourth Branch of Government* (New York: Vintage Books, 1965), p. 69.

[14]It is important that the student be able to distinguish between a pseudo-event and propaganda which has very different characteristics. *Pseudo-event:* Ambiguous truth, desire to be informed, synthetic facts, overcomplicated; *Propaganda:* appealing falsehood, willing to be influenced, opinions rather than facts, oversimplified. This is discussed in greater detail in Boorstin's article in *The Image*.

[15]Boorstin, *loc. cit.*

by the teacher that have thus far been fairly well omitted from study curriculums.

The Presidential Press Conference

One of the functions of the role of "watchdog" on government is maintaining a check on the actions of the President. This is accomplished in part by the presidential news conference which has become institutionalized since its informal inception in the days of Theodore Roosevelt. The progress of this institution has been arduous but persistent, hitting low points with the days of Hoover and riding its crest in the days of Franklin Delano Roosevelt. Truman marked his days in office with turbulent relations with the press, and Eisenhower's consistent noncommitments became well known. Kennedy took advantage of the use of television and projected a positive immage to both the press and the public.

Development of the various media has changed the tone of the press conference. It was formerly the sole responsibility of the news reporter to release and interpret the interview until the *New York Times* began to publish the text of the speech for public interpretation. Later, it became possible to release short transcripts to the radio. The entry of television and film cameras in 1955 compounded the already changing role of the press recorder; Douglas Cater presents the views of some critics:

> For some gloomy critics this latest development was the last straw, the final debasement of the conference as a profitable opportunity for communication with the President. Assuming that the reporter can get himself recognized, his question and the accompanying answer are formally transcribed, recorded, taped, and filmed. Almost before he can file his own copy both he and the President have been viewed on television screens all across the country. He has become, say these critics, an unpaid extra in a gigantic show. He has sold his birthright for a mess of publicity.[16]

The opposing view is: "By accommodating all the mass media, the President can more easily communicate with the citizenry. The press conference was never meant to be simply a special reserve for reporters."[17]

Essentially the conference follows the following general pattern: approximately two hundred reporters sit in a room awaiting the President; when he and his assistants arrive the questioning begins; reporters attempt to gain recognition by standing and addressing the President who randomly recognizes whom he wishes; the questions are not known to the President before the

[16]Cater, *op. cit.,* p. 41.
[17]*Ibid.,* p. 42.

meeting so he is literally "on the spot" and must deal with each probe as best he can. It is the pressmen who decide when the conference will come to a close and the stampede will begin out the door to contact the wireservices and individual newspapers.

This event has become an accepted tradition in American democracy. Responses are candid and a "no comment" may be as newsworthy as a direct answer to the question. Interesting topics for discussion in the classroom can be generated from a close look at the conference. For example, how much news is created as a result of unexpected questions (and answers)? What effect has the inception of the camera had on the interview? Has the conference become a vehicle for image creation rather than a source of the clarification of issues?

The Press and Congress

The press has developed a "working relationship" with some members of Congress. That is, there is a more intimate and, hence, first-hand knowledge of the activities of these men than with the Executive Branch of the government. Congressmen depend to a great extent on the interplay of news releases as a form of "feeler," for to them the news is a manipulative source of publicity for messages to both the public and constituents. It is an organizationally informal means of communication that has come to assume great significance in the everyday workings of the legislative process. Thus, the press and Congress have formed a seemingly "symbiotic relationship" each playing the role of "host" for the other in maintaining the balance.

Cater reports that senior reporters working on Capitol Hill experience a degree of intimacy with congressional leaders that junior statesmen seldom attain. He states, "At least once daily the wire-service representatives are invited in for sessions with the Speaker of the House and the Senate Majority Leader. On countless unnamed occasions the reporter may attend the informal convocations at which the earthier matters of politics are explored."[18]

What is the function, or dysfunction of this type of relationship when press responsibility is considered? What reciprocal demands are likely to emerge? How are loyalties and responsibilities perceived by members of the two groups, and the public?

One effect has been that this relationship requires that the press "overlook" some of the obvious, though "harmless," frauds committed each year by Congress. Carter found that, "Each year, for example, the House Appropriations Committee or one of its Subcommittees virtuously makes deep cuts in appropriations bills for funds already contractually obligated. Each year this action is duly rewarded by newspaper accounts that the Committee has 'slashed' the budget by such and such an amount. And later each year the

[18]*Ibid.*, p. 52.

Committee quietly restores the cut in its 'supplemental appropriations.' "[19] Apparently, though reporters are well aware of such actions, they do not care to take the initiative to report them to the public.

Free Press and Fair Trial

The rights and responsibilities of the press become a weighty problem when the question of the reporting of arrest and trial proceedings is concerned. While freedom of speech and press is to be jealously protected, the rights of the accused must be held equally as important. The disagreement that has arisen between the two agencies, the bar and the press, does not concern this generally stated problem, but it concerns the problem of to whom the assignment of the control of printed news is to be awarded: the bar association seeks lawful restrictions over the press, while newsmen and publishers resist relinguishment of any infringement on freedom of the press. Both groups, however, show a willingness to carefully assess the problem and come to a workable solution.

Serious and concerted action in the direction of cooperation was initiated by five media groups following the release of the Warren Commission Report (in which the blame for the killing of Lee Harvey Oswald was attributed in great part to both the Dallas Police Department and the news media). A committee, The Joint Media Committee on News Coverage Problems, met and produced a booklet suggesting the manner of treatment to be used in the reporting of an event. In December of 1966, the American Bar Association released a tentative draft of its committee, the Advisory Committee on Fair Trial and Free Press, to which the news media reacted with general favor but took exception to recommendations for official sanctioning of violation of the codes. In early 1967 the American Newspaper Association released its publication, *Free Press and Fair Trial,* in which it states that there is no real conflict between the First (free press) and Sixth (a speedy and public trial, by an impartial jury) Amendments, that news is not necessarily intrinsically prejudicial and finally basing its tenets on the "people's right to a free press" which it feels is a fundamental right not to be compromised by codes or covenants. The Bar of the City of New York issued its final report, *Freedom of the Press and Fair Trial,* calling for "voluntary controls," and furthermore stating that the courts could not claim power of control over information released by police or printed by the press. This appears to be a mutually workable compromise.

What has been apparently operant throughout this disagreement is the parallel, though not joint, efforts of the two agencies to resolve the admitted problem. The recognition has not been of universal agreement for it appears that more progress has been made at various state levels than at the national level where resistence to cooperation is more stringently maintained. It has been

[19]*Ibid.,* p. 56.

estimated also that nearly 50 percent of the states still lack impetus for cooperation, many refusing to admit a need for such a code.[20]

Governmental Releases

One well established, but little discussed, aspect of Washington reporting is the "leak" or "cloaked news." In this case the reporter has received a scoop or confidential release of news that, although released by a government representative, was done without official recognition. This is unattributed news, verging on rumor, as it is not possible to trace its origin. During times of stress in national decision making this a prime source of news. Cater says:

> Cloaked news has become an institutional practice in the conduct of modern government in Washington, part of the regular intercourse between government and the press. During periods of high tension when formal channels of communication such as the President's and the Secretary of State's press conferences are cut off, it often becomes the major means by which important news is transmitted.[21]

This type of news also takes the form of a background briefing where a few newsmen are called together in confidential tones by someone of official capacity, though it is not known until the final moment who has called the meeting together and for what purpose. The atmosphere is informal and social; the subject is broached cautiously, and there is an unspoken rule presiding that this official is merely talking things over and is not to be quoted. This rule requires compulsory plagarism; the journalist may use what he has learned only on his own authority. At best he may quote "informed circles" or "a high government spokesman."[22]

The leak has its obvious *raison d'être.* There is not only release from fixed responsibility, but this can be a means for personal debates between the varying points of view of officials without commitment. It can also be a means of testing new ideals before formal release to both colleagues and the public.

The "handout" is another aspect of prepared news. These are news releases that are given to reporters prior to the event it describes (though it is written in the past tense). Boorstin reports that, "the National Press Club in its Washington clubrooms has a large rack which is filled daily with the latest releases, so the reporter does not even have to visit the offices which gave them out."[23]

One problem involved with governmental releases lies in the perceived responsibilities of the press. Are they to be propaganda instruments for the

[20] Robert G. Kingsley, "Press-Bar Cooperation," *Freedom of Information Report*, No. 184 (July 1967).

[21] Cater, *op cit.*, p. 130.

[22] *Ibid.*, pp. 132-141.

[23] Boorstin, *op. cit.*, p. 19.

government or is their commitment to release all the facts to the public and pinpoint the responsibility for opinions and actions of officials? These forms of news release lend themselves to a high degree of distortion in the need for covering up a source or time span, thus leaving a high degree of manipulation to the reporter — to keep information from the public.

Some Influences on the Interpretations of News

The Reporter

The pressures that channel reporters' perception of an event are influenced by the organization that employs him. The news office has become increasingly bureaucratized, discouraging individuality in the interpretation of events. There has also been a reduction in job mobility of reporters, encouraging them to stay with one organization, rather than move from one job to another. Thus, the pressures of the higher echelon have become more significant and influential. Breed suggests that those values to which the reporter must adhere basically reflect the values prevailing in the society — middle class, conforming, and organization-man societies. These controls check some of the deviant actions that are called for by critics of the press.[24]

Warren Breed made a well-known study of social control in the newsroom. He found that bias still exists in spite of three empirical conditions that discourage the control of news. These discouraging conditions are: (1) publisher's policy sometimes contravenes journalistic norms; (2) staffers often personally disagree with it; and (3) executives cannot legitimately command that policy be followed. His study of the socio-cultural situation in the newsroom showed that the newsman's source of rewards is centered among his colleagues and superiors, rather than the readers, who are his assumed audience. He does not adhere to societal and professional ideals but rather redefines his values to the more pragmatic level of the newsroom group where he gains status rewards and the acceptance in a solidary group that is engaged in interesting, varied, and sometimes important work. He concludes, "Any important change toward a more 'free and responsible press' must stem from various possible pressures on the publisher, who epitomizes the policy-making and coordinating role."[25]

The Publisher

The bias of the publisher can be seen as a political influence when it is realized that there is not always a balancing of viewpoints from one source to

---

[24]Warren Breed, "Organizing the Media to Facilitate Discussion of Social Change," dittoed paper, Tulane University, 1966.

[25]Warren Breed, "Social Control in the Newsroom: A Functional Analysis," *Social Forces*, vol. 33 (1955), p. 335.

another. A poll taken by *Editor and Publisher,* a professional journal of the newspaper industry, showed the following political leanings of almost 80 percent of the total daily circulation of newspapers in the United States:[26]

Year	% Newspapers for GOP Candidate	% Newspapers for Dem. Candidate
1932	52	40
1936	57	36
1940	64	23
1944	60	22
1948	65	15
1952	67	15
1956	62	15
1960	57	16
1964	35	42

This imbalance can be tolerated if editorializing is restricted to the editorial page *and* the public is able to recognize it as such. Unfortunately, it has been found that readers of newspapers do not always distinguish between a newspaper's editorial policy and its coverage of news even when the paper tries to be impartial.[27]

News Management

Limitations of time and space are often convenient and plausible excuses for the differential handling and selection of news. Ruth Love found, however, that differential news treatment existed during the reporting of the Kennedy assassination during which neither time nor space was a problem, for the entire weekend was devoted to continuous news releases on the events as they unfolded; the problem was rather one of "time fill." The differential treatment in this case was caused more by "taste and discretion.." There was differential handling of the key figures; much discretion was used in the news coverage of Jacqueline Kennedy, while there were no holds barred concerning Lee Harvey Oswald.[28]

[26] *Freedom of Information Report,* No. 145, (1965).
[27] Sidney S. Goldfish, "How Editors Use Research on the Minneapolis Dailies," *Journalism Quarterly,* vol. 37 (1960), pp. 365-372.
[28] Ruth Leeds Love, "Social Control in Newscasting: The Case of TV Coverage of the Kennedy Assassination." Paper delivered at the American Sociological Association, 1965.

Another form of news management by the government and the press occurred during the Cuban Invasion of 1961. Neal Houghton found that there was increasing hostility of our press and leadership for more than a year prior to the invasion. The pattern found was: (1) Castro has perverted his revolution; (2) he has abandoned his concern for his people; (3) he has talked nastily to and about our political personalities; (4) he has taken American property; (5) our government has shown remarkable "patience" and "forbearance" in it all; (6) the time is approaching for drastic action; and (7) Communism must not be allowed to get a foothold in this hemisphere – only 90 miles from our shore.[29] The questions that arise here are, how much evidence was presented to back these accusations, and were they merely a conditioning of the American public to a prescribed mode of action by the government, aided by the press?

Management of the news was embarrassingly evident to Adlai Stevenson as he stood at the United Nations meeting following his denial of United States involvement in the invasion. He was quoted in the *New York Times* on April 18 as saying:

Dr. Roa has charged the United States with aggression against Cuba and invasion coming from Florida. These charges are totally false and I deny them categorically. The United States has committed no aggression against Cuba and no offensive has been launched from Florida or from any other part of the United States.[30]

The Bay of Pigs invasion was launched on April 17, the day prior to this speech.

Jack Backer studied thirteen members of the "prestige press" to determine how concerned they were about the control and management of the news by the administration during and after the Cuban crisis and found that the reasons may be attributed to:

1. Newspaper officials believe that the problem is for the press and that airing the discussion in newspapers would not help the situation.
2. Editors in the home offices are less concerned about news management than are the reporters who face the problem(s) in their daily work.
3. Newspapers hesitate to take a stand because they are too concerned with charges that monopoly newspapers present only one side of an issue.
4. Newspaper officials feel there is a need for a rethinking of the traditional relationships between government and the press in a free society.[31]

[29] Neal D. Houghton, "The Cuban Invasion of 1961 and the U.S. Press, In Retrospect." *Journalism Quarterly*, vol. 42 (1964), p. 422.

[30] *Ibid.* (as quoted from the *New York Times*, April 18, 1961), p. 428.

[31] Jack Backer, "The 'Prestige Press' and News Management in the Cuban Crisis," *Journalism Quarterly*, vol. 41 (1964), p. 265.

The Recipient of News

The Concept of the Audience

The communicator has some image of his audience when he formulates and communicates his message; however, due to the usually stratified makeup of that audience it is often amorphous and artificial.

Though the communicator may actually be addressing himself to someone other than the manifest audience, the major reference group being colleagues, superiors, critics, or creators in other fields; the audience image does hold some concern when it is in obvious conflict with his self-perceived role of communicator. Creators of messages must please an aggregate of persons in varying positions, each of which may alter the structure of the final product. Each new product thus becomes a gamble.[32]

As has been discussed, the audience, or individual recipient of communications, does not accept a message at "face value," but rather has predispositions that are formed by present and past group memberships that work as a filtering system. To complicate matters further, if a medium or communicator is viewed as unfair in relation to an area that is highly salient to that individual, he will transfer this distrust to other messages transmitted by that medium or communicator.[33]

When a message is received and accepted by the audience, it must be reinforced by group support and interpersonal communication to be retained as a significant bit of information. The relation of mass communications to interpersonal communications is variable, though Bradley Greenberg has found a recurring pattern in the diffusion of a news event. The relationship was found to be:

1. The mass media were the most pervasive first source of information across seventeen different news events studied.
2. For bulletin or major news events, the broadcast media predominate as first sources of information. For lesser events as measured by their dissemination, the newspaper is the principal first source of information.
3. Interpersonal communication is most active as a first source of information in the diffusion of events attended to by nearly everyone or by nearly no one.
4. When a news event is of near-epic or crisis proportion interpersonal

---

[32] Herbert Gans, "The Creater-Audience Relationship in the Mass Media,"

[33] Jack Lyle, "Religion and Politics as Mediators of Perceived Bias in Competing Newspapers," U.C.L.A. (Mimeographed), 1965.

channels of communication are as important as the mass media in disseminating initial information.[34]

The mass media remains an important factor whether information is learned from it directly or through interpersonal communications, for it is still the only original source for most political information. Unfortunately, it appears that there are few ways that the individual can resist the media short of avoidance. C. Wright Mills has suggested three possible means: (1) so long as the media are not completely monopolized, he can play one off against another; (2) the individual can compare what is said on the media with his own personal experience and direct knowledge of events; (3) individuals may gain points of resistance against the mass media by the comparison of experience of opinions among themselves.[35]

These are possible topics for discussion, which become even more relevant when coupled with considerations of: the increased centralization of power in the media through mergers, the media as a single source of information on foreign affairs, and the decreasing tendency to discuss issues in small groups. The student should become aware of the role of the audience in the process of the flow of information; he should know when the individual is vulnerable and when not. He should examine means of resistence (other than avoidance) and change, if he disagrees with the existing situation.

Enculturation

The mass entertainment media have been accused of being "bland" or organizing their content so as to be inoffensive to the greatest number of the population. It has been said that "to please is desirable – not to offend is imperative." The media attempt, in general, to maintain the status quo in societal values and resist deviance and change. Their presentation of any form of deviation from the general norm is by setting it in a brackground of disapproval, "crime does not pay," the "good guy always wins," and the like. The preferential values are those of the "happy medium." Studies of entertainment media show the preferential treatment of groups and norms that represent white, middle-class, "protestant-ethic" standards. Frank Gentile and S. M. Miller found that middle-class characters dominate the television screen while working-class characters are but a small percentage of the characters seen in their study. When working-class persons were portrayed, they were mainly seen in melodramas. The portrayals were dominated by negative characteristics in general, though the

---

[34] Bradley S. Greenberg, "Person-to-Person Communication in the Diffusion of a Newsevent," *Journalism Quarterly,* vol. 41 (1964), pp. 489-494.

[35] Mills, *op. cit.,* p. 591-593.

pattern was often that of a progression from negative at the beginning to positive by the completion of the program.[36]

Johns-Heine and Gerth studied the values in mass periodical fiction, finding a shift over the years that depicted the "ideal" middle-class hero and setting.[37] Berelson and Slater found in their study of majority and minority American depiction in magazine fiction that the "Americans" received both greater qualitative and quantitative preferential treatment in frequency, role, delineation, status and goals than minority or foreign groups. The Anglo-Saxon/Nordic received better treatment the closer they adhered to the American norm.[38]

Some forms of media that are regarded as entertainment are also politico-socio-enculturators. Most people have come to realize that the "funnies" are not just "funny." Many comic strips, such as "Mary Worth" and "Rex Morgan, M.D.," have definite moral lessons, each episode carries a lesson on how to be "nice" and very "middle-class" in perspective. "Little Orphan Annie," which has declined in popularity and coverage, is imbued with political and social significance. Al Capp is perhaps the most controversial cartoonist of the day, primarily because of his apparent switch in point-of-view from a liberal perspective to the now conservative leaning.[39]

Narcotizing Dysfunction

Lazarsfeld and Merton add two effects of the mass media to that of enculturation. First is the immediate effect of "status conferral," whereby when an individual is singled out by the media as a communicator he has attention drawn to him (or his group) and his status is thereby legitimized. This occurs through a recognition that one's stance must be significant to have been singled out from the large, anonymous masses for public notice.

More significant is the second, "formal literacy," a latent effect that tends to sterilize the traditional democratic model of the formation of public opinion. The rise of popular education has created an ability to read and grasp crude ideas, but where there is little conceptualization or relation deeper mean-

[36] Frank Gentile and S. M. Miller, "Television and Social Class," *Sociology and Social Research*, vol. 45 (1961), pp. 259-264.

[37] P. Johns-Heine and H. Gerth, "Values in Mass Periodical Fiction," *Public Opinion Quarterly*, vol. 13 (1949), pp. 105-113.

[38] Bernard Berelson and P. Slater, "Majority and Minority Americans: An Analysis of Magazine Fiction," *Public Opinion Quarterly*, vol. 10 (1946), pp. 108-197.

[39] Some of the studies conducted are A. Lyle W. Shannon, "The Opinions of Little Orphan Annie and Her Firends," *Public Opinion Quarterly*, vol. 18 (1954), pp. 169-179; B. D. Auster, "A Content Analysis of 'Little Orphan Annie,' " *Social Problems*, vol. 2 (1954), pp. 26-33; and C. Arnold Rose, "Mental Health Attitudes of Youth as Influenced by a Comic Strip," (a study of "Rex Morgan, M.D."), *Journalism Quarterly*, vol. 35 (1953), pp. 333-342.

ings; "people read more and understand less." This creates a superficial rather than real concern for societal problems. The flood of information to which the individual is exposed each day tends to "narcotize" rather than "energize" him. The individual receives information and may even intellectualize it — think of alternate solutions — but takes no concerted action in relation to it. He:

> Takes his secondary contact with the world of political reality, his reading and listening and thinking, as a vicarious performance . . . . He comes to mistake *knowing* about problems of the day for *doing* something about them. His social conscience remains spotlessly clean. He *is* concerned. He *is* informed. And he has all sorts of ideas as to what should be done. But, after he has gotten through his dinner and after he has listened to his favored radio programs and after he has read his second newspaper of the day, it is really time for bed.[40]

They conclude that these large doses of mass communication have transformed the energies of men from active participation into passive knowledge.

Summary and Conclusions

The study of mass communication has thus far been essentially ignored in secondary social studies classrooms. Textbooks show little concern for the media as a study focus and teachers have not been adequately prepared in their training to supplement where the textbook falls short. It has been the aim of this chapter to touch upon some of the possible problem areas that exist and could reasonably be used as subjects of inquiry.

The news media were differentiated into newspapers, magazines, television, and radio, each of which were shown to have unique problems. The question of an adequate definition of "news" was approached, drawing few conclusions beyond agreement that news is a transient or fragile knowledge about an event.

Of the different forms of news, the pseudo-event has been emphasized as a study focus because of its close relation to political events. Examples of this type of news were: the presidential press conference, congressional relations with the press, the role of the press in the reporting of trial news, and governmental releases.

Additional pressures that shape the flow of news once the event has been recorded have been briefly discussed in relation to the perception of the reporter, the publisher, the government, and other agencies that "manage" the news. The recipients of news — the audiences — were briefly mentioned

---

[40]Paul Lazarsfeld and Robert Merton, "Mass Communication, Popular Taste and Organized Social Action," in S. Bryson, ed., *The Communication of Ideas* (Harper & Row, Publishers, 1948), pp. 95-118.

describing some of the influences that operate in interpreting the news received. The attempt has been, then, to suggest some of the many approaches to the study of mass communication. Additional information on these and other approaches can be found by reading the full reports of the studies mentioned and the recommended references in the bibliography at the end of the chapter.

Addendum

Book	No. Pages on Media	No. Pages in Book	Quality of Coverage	Subjects in Coverage
Citizenship in Action, Fred B. Painter and Harold H. Bixler, Charles Scribner's Sons, 1958	2½	585	fair	How news is placed in the printed media; role of the wire service; how to choose a good newspaper or magazine.
American Government, Robert P. Ludlum, et al. Houghton Mifflin Company, 1965	2	625	poor	How officials hold press conferences to influence voters; FCC controls; presidential free use of TV.
Goals of Democracy, Samuel P. McCutchen, et al, The Macmillan Company, 1962	3	648	fair	Brief discussion of bias in newspapers; mentions magazines; themes of movies; number of books printed; FCC controls; Hitler's and FDR's use of radio.
Our Changing Social Order, Ruth Wood Gavian and Robert Rienow, D.C. Heath & Company, 1964	7	457	fair to good	Getting information on public affairs; lists criteria for a "good" newspaper; brief discussion of magazines; FCC controls; socializing influences.
Background of World Affairs, Julia Emery, The World Publishing Company, 1950	9	372	fair to good (but outdated)	Different flow of news through different media; how press services operate; varying attitudes of books; structure of newscasters.
Modern Sociology, Marvin R. Koller and Harold C. Couse, Holt, Rinehart & Winston, Inc., 1965	3+	299	fair	Discussion of H.G. Wells' "War of the Worlds"; some WWII propaganda techniques; mention of some possible effects of the media; advertising; political use in image formation (Nixon and JFK); bland content of TV.
Sociology, Paul H. Landis, Ginn and Company, 1965	3+	485	poor to fair	Techniques of advertisers; brief discussion of availability of audience; mention of TV as a status symbol; FDR and the Great Debates.
American Government in Today's World, Robert Rienow, D.C. Heath & Company, 1962 (revised)	3	713	poor	Presidential use of the press; radio and TV as entertainment rather than opinion molders; FCC control.
Government in our Republic, Stuart G. Brown and Charles L. Peltier, The Macmillan Company, 1967	4	736	fair	Warns of news slanting; newspaper chains; brief mention of movies; control of the media in the USSR

Annotated Bibliography

Emery, W., *Broadcasting and Government: Responsibilities and Regulations.* Michigan State University Press, 1961. A source for understanding aspects of broadcasting in relation to the Government. Includes a primer of laws, rules and regulations of the Federal Communications Commission and covers all aspects of governmental control of broadcasting.

Farace, Vincent, and Dohohew, Lewis, "Mass Communication in National Social Systems: A Study of 43 Variables in 115 Countries," *Journalism Quarterly*, 37 (1960), 253-261. A study of the variables usually found to be related to the degree of freedom allowed in a national press.

Ferry, W. H., and Ashmore, Harry S., *Mass Communication.* Center for the Study of Democratic Institutions (Fund for the Republic), 1966. A discussion of the United States press by fourteen foreign journalists, a discussion by Center staff members, and articles by Ferry and Ashmore.

Friedson, Eliot, "Communication Research and the Concept of the Mass," *American Sociological Review,* 18 (1953), 313-317. A definition of the "audience" and a consideration of the categorization of a "mass grouping."

Gans, Herbert, "The Mass Media as an Educational Institution," *The Urban Review,* 2 (1967), 5-10. A comparison is made between the schools and the mass media as two significant socializing institutions that dominate children's lives; he considers the questions of how well children learn what the two offer them and how well they learn what they need to know to live in an adult society?

Gieber, Walter, "News is What Newspapermen Make It," in Lewis A. Dexter and David M. White (eds.), *People, Society and Mass Communications.* Free Press of Glencoe, Inc., New York, 1964, pp. 173-182. A discussion of the factors influencing the selection and reporting of news; the flow from source to reporter and newsgathering bureaucracy to the public.

Gregg, J., "Newspaper Editoral Endorsements and California Elections, 1948-62," *Journalism Quarterly,* 42 (1965), 532-538. A study of the editorial endorsements of eleven California newspapers; comparisons with voting results show the influence of the endorsements, particularly at the local levels and on lengthy ballots.

Hansen, Donald A. and Parsons, J. Herschel, *Mass Communication: A Research Bibliography.* The Glendessary Press, 1968. A listing of over 3,000 references divided into major subject areas emphasizing materials for the researcher but including many areas of study for the teacher interested in general background.

Klapper, J., "Social Effects of Mass Communications," in W. Schramm (ed.), *The Science of Human Communication.* Basic Books, Inc., Publishers, New York, 1963, pp. 65-76. A consideration of different points of view: mass communication versus personal influence, television's influence on children, and the possible effects of propaganda.

Kraus, Sidney, "The Political Use of Television," *Journal of Broadcasting,* 8 (1964), 219-228. Two uses of television in political communication debates and computer prediction during election coverage are explored.

Lang, Kurt, and Lang, Gladys, "The Unique Perspective of Television and Its Effect," *Social Problems,* 4 (1956), 107-116. A differentiation is made here between political participation in an organized setting and "living politics at a distance"; a discussion of active versus passive action.

Larsen, Otto, Gray, Louis, and Fortis, J. Gerald, "Goals and Goal-Achievement Methods in Television Content: Models for Anomie?," *Sociological Inquiry,* 33 (1963), 180-196. This is an attempt to explore through content analysis, the goals, methods of goal achievement, and combinations of goals and methods that are presented on television. A discussion of anomie as portrayed on dramatic programs.

Lippmann, Walter, *Public Opinion.* The Macmillan Company, New York, 1922. A discussion of the growth and development of public opinion in a democracy.

Maccoby, Eleanor, "Effects of the Mass Media," in M. Hoffman and L. Hoffman (eds.), *Review of Child Development Research,* 1 (Russell Sage Foundation, 1964), 323-348. A discussion of the methodological problems involved in isolating the effects of mass media. Findings are summarized from existing studies, emphasizing the results from studies in which data were obtained before and after the advent of television.

McLuhan, M., *Understanding Media: The Extension of Man.* McGraw-Hill Book Company, New York, 1964. A philosophical discussion of the implications of the electronic age of communication. This book extends its discussion beyond consideration of the mass media.

Mendelsohn, Harold, "Sociological Perspectives on the Study of Mass Communication," in Lewis A. Dexter and David M. White (eds.), *People, Society and Mass Communications.* Free Press of Glencoe, Inc., New York, 1964, pp. 29-36. A discussion of three basic perspectives: Communication as an essential process of the social system, mass communication as it affects attitudes and values, and a demise of power nation of mass communication.

Merton, Robert K., "Introduction: Wissenssoziologie and Mass Communications," in R. Merton (ed.), *Social Theory and Social Structure.* Free Press of Glencoe, Inc., New York, 1957, pp. 439-455. A comparison of sociological research in America and Europe using mass communication research as an example. This is a rigorous article for one who is unfamiliar with discussions of theory but a valuable background source.

Peterson, T., "From Mass Media to Class Media," in Lewis A. Dexter and David M. White (eds.), *People, Society and Mass Communications.* Free Press of Glencoe, Inc., New York, 1964, pp. 250-259. This chapter discusses the effects of television on the amount and kind of reading that occurs. It also suggests the competitive motives behind the attempts to change the situation.

Riley, J., and Riley, M., "Mass Communication and the Social System," in R. K. Merton *et al.* (eds.), *Sociology Today.* Basic Books. Inc., Publishers, New York, 1959, pp. 537-579. This discusses Laswell's paradigm, "Who says what in which channel to whom with what effect," and extends its boundaries. A good background in the theory of mass communication research.

Rose, Arnold, "The Study of the Influence of the Mass Media on Public Opinion," *Kyklos,* 15 (1962), 465-482. An historical discussion that covers the media of the twenties to the present, showing how a theoretical approach developed.

Schramm, W., Lyle, J., and Parker, E., *Television in the Lives of Our Children.* Stanford University Press, 1961. An analysis of the effects of television on children based on a study of over 6,000 children, with information obtained from approximately 2,300 parents, teachers, and school officials.

Siebert, Fred, Peterson, Theodore, and Schramm, Wilbur, *Four Theories of The Press.* University of Illinois Press. 1956. A theoretical discussion and definition of four distinct approaches to the concept of the role of the press in a society.

Wright, Charles, "Functional Analysis and Mass Communication," *Public Opinion Quarterly,* 24 (1960), 605-620. A discussion that emphasizes the importance of viewing mass communication as functioning within the larger sociological perspective of the culture, social organizations and human groups; uses a case study approach.

PART IV

The Behavioral Sciences and the Humanities: Interdisciplinary Approaches to the New Social Studies

The humanities, especially in the form of history, have had a great deal of influence on the traditional social studies curriculum. Recent indications are, however, that the behavioral sciences will play an important role in future social studies courses. At any rate, the humanities and the social sciences, and especially the behavioral sciences, are crucial areas in the social studies now that the revolution in social studies education has occurred and forces are being mustered to influence the social studies of the future. The state of tomorrow's social studies programs cannot now be known, but it would be accurate to say that neither the humanities nor the social sciences will exclude the other from having a part in that future. It is therefore incumbent on historians, social scientists, social studies educators, and social studies teachers to explore approaches which will effectively employ both the humanities and the social sciences. The following chapters constitute the beginning efforts of a social studies educator to relate the humanities and the social sciences to each other in the social studies curriculum.

CHAPTER 7

History, the Social Sciences, and Comparative Approaches in the Social Studies

Dale L. Brubaker

Dale L. Brubaker is Assistant Professor of Social Science Education at the University of California, Santa Barbara. He is author of Alternative Directions for the Social Studies, *editor of* Innovation in the Social Studies, *and co-editor with R. Murray Thomas and Lester B. Sands of the book* Strategies for Curriculum Change: Cases from Thirteen Nations.

Introduction

The use of comparisons is part of our intellectual heritage. Aristotle and Montesquieu, for example, were very much concerned with the relationship between ways of life and ways of governing. Likewise, many contemporary scholars use comparisons in their research and teaching.

It would be inappropriate to suggest that secondary social studies teachers and students engage in highly sophisticated research activities based on various comparative approaches; to suggest that such approaches may be employed as a useful didactic device in teaching secondary social studies is quite another matter. The latter suggestion is the basis for this chapter.

Characteristics of the Use of Comparisons

Two major steps are usually involved in the use of comparisons:

1) How does x differ from y?   and/or
   How are x and y similar?
2) Why are they different?   and/or
   Why are they similar?

Step 1) is relatively easy to answer compared to Step 2) for it is in explaining the why of a matter that one is led to multiple causation. The question of whether or not a comparison is a fruitful one to make is certainly legitimate and may lend itself to a more circuitous paradigm or working model as follows:

1) How does x differ from y?   and/or
   How are x and y similar?
2) What is the significance, if any, of a similarity and/or difference? (The teacher's tone of voice, facial expression, and general bearing will demonstrate whether or not he seriously feels the question is worth exploring.)
3) Is there information, for example, previously conducted research, relevant to the subject?
4) Why are they different?   and/or
   Why are they similar?

The second part of the paradigm is most relevant to the social studies teacher. The teacher and his students must work together to establish the criteria for the selection of phenomena to be compared. For example, the comparison of apples and oranges makes little sense unless they are compared on the basis of a common characteristic such as each containing the seeds for its own proliferation or each containing vitamin content beneficial to the individual who eats the fruit. In either case, the person making the comparison is looking for characteristics common to the two phenomena. A more appropriate example for the social studies teacher would be for the teacher to look for characteristics common to both Negroes and Caucasians with the idea of having students work for the harmony of all races. The teacher has "stacked the cards" in the interest of what many would consider to be a humane cause.

The teacher may also accentuate differences between phenomena to achieve his objective. For example, if his students ostracize a member of the class for his poorly made clothes the teacher may point out that tolerance for differences is a basic tenet of democracy and students should learn to appreciate each other's idiosyncrasies.

The two examples, searching for similarities between Negroes and Caucasians, and isolating differences between students' preferences, are quite interesting; for the teacher's primary objective in both cases is the same—to have all people get along together. Yet the teacher uses different tacks to achieve his preconceived goal.

A third approach would be for a teacher to have his students look for both similarities and differences between Negroes and Caucasians on the basis of characteristics chosen by the students themselves. Where this would lead would not be predetermined and would probably be more time consuming. Yet, this approach would seem to be more intellectually honest.

The process of making comparisons often leads one to the formation of value judgments. For example, it is a fact that apples and oranges bear the seeds for their own proliferation. Yet it would be more common to hear a student make the following comparison: "I like apples more than oranges," or "I like oranges more than apples." In either case, a value judgment has been made on the basis of the personal preference or taste of the individual. Although it is likely that some other student will challenge the first student's value judgment, it is not likely that the argument will be resolved. Student A may say that he likes apples better than oranges for reasons *X, Y,* and *Z* and Student B may respond that he likes oranges better than apples for reasons *X, Y,* and *Z.* Then Students A and B may argue about the validity of each other's reasons.

Yet with the matter of one's attitudes toward Negroes, other dimensions exist. For the purposes of the social studies it is not enough to say that my personal preference is to like or dislike Negroes. Students and teachers must establish ground rules which will help them get to the issues involved in the various relationships between Negroes and Caucasians in the particular society we have in the United States or particular social systems in the United States. The ground rules previously referred to will consist of a list of priorities as to the most valid tools of analysis to be used in dealing with a particular issue. For example, the students and teacher may agree that intuition is less valid than empirical findings or that Students A and B have so much at stake with a particular issue—e.g. open occupancy in housing—that their testimonials are probably less objective than those of more detached analysts.

It can be seen from the previous discussion that comparisons are used in attempting to clarify resemblances and differences displayed by phenomena (or classes of phenomena) considered, on the basis of certain criteria, to be comparable.[1] Although the use of comparisons is common to many disciplines, there is some controversy as to whether or not there is such a thing as *the comparative method.*[2] It is readily apparent that a problem of categorization

[1] The complete definition is as follows: "Comparative method is a general term denoting the procedures which, by clarifying the resemblances and differences displayed by phenomena (or classes of phenomena) deemed, on various criteria, to be 'comparable', aim at eliciting and classifying (a) causal factors in the emergence and development of such phenomena (or classes); (b) patterns of interrelation both within and between such phenomena (or classes)." Julius Gould, "Comparative Method," in Julius Gould and William L. Kolb, eds., *A Dictionary of the Social Sciences* (New York: Free Press of Glencoe, Inc., 1964), p. 116.

[2] Oscar Lewis, for example, contends that there is no distinctive comparative method in anthropology as ". . .the method of a comparison is only one aspect of comparison, other relevant aspects being the aims or objectives, the content, and the location in space of the entities compared." Oscar Lewis, "Comparisons in Cultural Anthropology," in F. W. Moore, ed., *Readings in Cross-Cultural Methodology* (New York: Human Relations Area Files, 1966), p. 50. Lewis's criticism of the use of the term, comparative method, seems justified. This is why the present author has used the term comparative approaches rather than the comparative method.

exists in relation to the use of comparisons in various academic disciplines. Certain areas of a discipline use comparisons; others do not. Certain scholars within an area of a discipline use comparisons; others do not. Some schools of thought within a discipline support the use of comparisons; others do not.

The Use of Comparisons in History and the Social Sciences

It is the intent of the following paragraphs to demonstrate how comparisons have been used in history and the social sciences—the disciplines which form the basic structure from which the social studies draws its strength. If it can be demonstrated that these disciplines have seriously attempted to use comparisons, then we can assert that there is an intellectually honest basis for comparative approaches in the social studies.

Let us first consider the disciplines of history and anthropology as there are indications that these two disciplines may very well play the leading role in future social studies courses.[3]

Political historians of the mid-nineteenth century used the comparative method to trace institutional relationships and origins. A major advantage, according to those who used the method, was that it would help reduce racial, political, and national prejudices.[4] At present, historians use comparisons as an analytical device primarily to see the similarities and differences in various interpretations of history. At this point one of the most advantageous uses of the comparative approach for social studies students is apparent: "The comparative study of differing interpretations of historians can be a fascinating motivation for the study of history."[5]

Historians are more cautious in using comparisons, however, than are many social scientists. A clue to the explanation of this may be found in the historian's emphasis on the uniqueness of events.

Teachers who try to use the inquiry into the past for a better understanding of the present must remember that a comparison of present conditions with similar conditions in the past is not enough. Similarities between the past and the present are important—but so are the differences. Without the understanding of these differences there can be no history

---

[3] Paul D. Hines, "World History," in C. Benjamin Cox and Byron G. Massialas, eds., *Social Studies in the United States: A Critical Appraisal* (New York: Harcourt, Brace & World, Inc., 1967), p. 213.

[4] Edward N. Saveth, "The Conceptualization of American History," in Edward N. Saveth, ed., *American History and the Social Sciences* (New York: Free Press of Glencoe, Inc., 1964), pp. 10-11.

[5] Mark M. Krug, *History and the Social Sciences* (Waltham, Mass.: Blaisdell Publishing Co., Inc., 1967), pp. 18-19.

because the concept of change is a basic and valuable historical principle.[6]

Some historians (incidentally, those most lauded by the new "inquiry group" in social studies education) criticize their colleagues for not relying more on the behavioral sciences in general and not using comparative study in particular. David M. Potter and Thomas C. Cochran are but two examples of historians who wish to draw on the behavioral sciences. Cochran feels that history ". . .should not only record the achievements of the past, but also try to find analogies to a confused present."[7] Cochran advocates cross-cultural comparisons as an avenue to the upgrading of historical scholarship. Potter's work is discussed in Chapter 8 of this book.

If comparative approaches are adopted by the social studies, anthropology will probably play the leading role for ". . .the singular characteristic of the anthropological method is *comparison.*"[8] According to Margaret Mead, "All cultural analysis is comparative. It is assumed that without comparison culture would be imperceptible to the individual who would not be able to distinguish between cultural behavior and biologically given, unlearned behavior."[9] Anthropology has an immediate fascination for most social studies students for the cross-cultural subject matter is "unusual" and "different." Anthropologist Pertti J. Pelto states, "When a thirst for systematic observation and comparative research are grafted onto the earlier romantic impulses, the motivations for a mature anthropology begin to emerge."[10] Motivations for such a mature anthropology may be initiated in the social studies curriculum of the future.

Although many contemporary sociologists are disillusioned with the comparative method, there was a time when the comparative method was the par excellence of sociology. The method was first used by the evolutionist sociologists such as Emile Durkheim. One major problem in using comparisons in sociology is that of defining the unit of comparison. The problem leads many sociologists to feel that comparative studies lack the necessary rigor when conducted cross culturally but have value when restricted to investigations within particular societies. "Much recent sociological research has concentrated on testing limited hypotheses by small scale comparisons, e.g. connections between urban living and divorce or delinquency rates, between family size and social mobility, between social class and educational attainment, etc."[11]

---

[6]*Ibid.,* p. 24.

[7] Thomas C. Cochran, *The Inner Revolution* (New York: Harper Torchbooks, 1964), p. 185.

[8] Bruce R. Joyce, *Strategies for Elementary Social Science Education* (Chicago: Science Research Associates, Inc., 1965), p. 47.

[9] *The Study of Culture at a Distance,* Margaret Mead and Rhoda Metraux, eds. (Chicago: University of Chicago Press, 1953), p. 26.

[10]Pertti J. Pelto, *The Study of Anthropology* (Columbus, Ohio: Charles E. Merrill Books, Inc., 1965), p. 5.

[11] T.B. Bottomore, *Sociology* (Englewood Cliffs, N.J.: Prentice-Hall, Inc., 1962), p. 50. The comparative study of ethnic stratification is advocated by Tamotsu Shibutani and Kian

Comparisons are very important to the discipline of economics. "A primary task of economics," according to economists Richard S. Martin and Reuben G. Miller, "is to explain both the essential similarities and the nature of the differences in the economic life of different peoples, so that man may be better able to understand the conditions under which he lives and the alternatives that are open to him."[12] This kind of explanation is not confined to a course entitled "Comparative Economic Systems" but is valuable in any social studies course.

No longer do American political scientists simply describe foreign governments, comparisons with the United States political system being implied rather than stated. "Contemporary political scientists compare institutions, such as parties or legislatures; processes, such as those of socialization or conflict-resolution; and even whole political systems."[13] Comparisons have expanded beyond the Western world to the non-Western political systems so that in the words of political scientist Francis J. Sorauf, ". . .the comparers are in many ways the new 'general theorists' of political science."[14] The implications for less parochial courses in the social studies curriculum are obvious.

Raymond H. Muessig and Vincent R. Rogers want to draw the attention of social studies students to a basic problem important to all geographers: What is the nature of the relationship between man and his environment?[15] To study this question students may well profit from an examination of geographic theories which have sought to explain this relationship. Geographer Jan O. M. Broek suggests that a comparison of the following viewpoints, or theories, will help the student better comprehend the nature of geography: geography as biophysical science; geography as nature-man relationships; geography as human ecology; geography as landscape study; geography as the study of distributions; and geography as theory of earth space.[16] This kind of study by social studies students would demonstrate the many and diverse routes of inquiry which geographers follow; students would also see that geographic understanding is proximate, or tentative, rather than definitive.

It should now be evident that the use of comparisons is an enterprise which has been taken seriously in all of the social sciences and history. It is the

---

M. Kwan in their book, *Ethnic Stratification* (New York: The Macmillian Company, 1965), p. 21. Stanislav Andreski's book, *Elements of Comparative Sociology* (London: Weidenfield and Nicolson, 1964), may also be of interest to the reader. Andreski advocates use of the comparative method in modern sociological studies.

[12] Richard S. Martin and Teuben G. Miller, *Economics* (Columbus, Ohio: Charles E. Merrill Books, Inc., 1965), p. 9.

[13] Francis J. Sorauf, *Political Science* (Columbus, Ohio: Charles E. Merrill Books, Inc., 1965), p. 36.

[14] *Ibid.*, p. 37.

[15] Jan O.M. Broek, *Geography* (Columbus, Ohio: Charles E. Merrill Books, Inc., 1965), p. 113.

[16] *Ibid.*, pp. 76-79.

thesis of this chapter that the use of comparisons and analogies may have important heuristic value for social studies students. That is, comparisons and analogies will aid critical thinking by being useful investigative devices.[17] The remainder of this chapter is devoted to a discussion of various ways in which comparative approaches may be employed in social studies classes.

Employing Comparative Approaches in the Social Studies

Comparative approaches may be used in four main ways in the social studies curriculum: (1) as the basis for the entire secondary social studies curriculum so that each course would be based on an overall comparative scheme; (2) as the basis for a particular course in the social studies curriculum such as world history; (3) as a basis for a unit within a course in the social studies curriculum; and (4) as an approach to be used on an occasional basis, usually in a spontaneous way.

Comprehensive Comparative Approaches

The best known attempt to build an entire social studies curriculum around the comparative approach is described in the book, *Improving the Teaching of World Affairs*. The Glens Falls Story is told by Harold M. Long, Director of the ITWA Program, and Robert N. King, Director of Instruction in Glens Falls, New York. The Glens Falls Project was a ". . .deliberate and systematic effort to deepen and broaden understanding of certain key generalizations by providing cumulative experiences from grades one through twelve."[18] The orientation is closer to the behavioral sciences than to history for as historian Edwin Fenton notes, ". . .most historians are not comfortable with concepts."[19] Concepts or generalizations and experiences which supported the learning of such generalizations are quoted at length in the following paragraphs to give the reader a more comprehensive picture of the Glens Falls Project.

Generalization, essentially geographic in nature: "The world is shrinking in distance and time."

[17]Jerome Bruner recognized this in including the use of analogy as a general heuristic rule. Jerome S. Bruner, *The Process of Education* (New York: Vintage Books, 1960), p. 64. See also: C. Benjamin Cox, "American History," *Social Studies in the United States: A Critical Appraisal* (New York: Harcourt, Brace & World, Inc., 1967), pp. 71-72.

[18]Harold M. Long and Robert N. King, *Improving the Teaching of World Affairs* (Washington, D.C.: National Council for the Social Studies Bulletin No. 35, 1964), pp. 30-31.

[19]Edwin Fenton, "A Structure of History," in Irving Morrissett, ed., *Concepts and Structure in the New Social Studies Curricula* (West Lafayette, Ind.: Social Science Education Consortium, Inc., 1966), p. 52.

A first grade class discovers that a bus ride downtown takes only three minutes, whereas it takes fifteen minutes to walk the same distance.

A third grade class learns that a jet plane can make the ten-week voyage of Columbus in six hours.

A sixth grade class reads that flight over the North Pole brings Moscow as close to Chicago as it is to New York City.

A junior high school class in arithmetic computes the changes involved in flying through several time zones.

A senior high school biology class learns that the outbreak of a tropical disease may be as close as the nearest airport.

Generalization, essentially economic in nature: "Food, clothing, and shelter are basic needs of all human beings."

A first grade class studies homes and foods of children in other lands.

A third grade class studying India uses a film that shows that many people are living on a bare subsistence level, and that this is influencing their health, education, and happiness.

A fifth grade class studies how the wealth and welfare of Norway relate to the way basic human needs are met in food, occupations, shelter, and recreation.

A junior high school class in social studies learns about community dependence on world markets.

A senior high school class in American history debates the question of foreign aid to underdeveloped countries.

A senior high school class in secretarial practice uses motion picture films to learn about free enterprise systems in various countries.

Generalization, essentially social in nature: "A knowledge of cultures of other nations contributes to better communication and international understanding."

A second grade class learns some of the songs sung by French school children.

A physical education class learns to dance the *kolo,* or *sieben schrutt.*

A fourth grade class studies the contributions of European scientists to American science, and vice versa.

A sixth grade class makes a list of American words derived from foreign languages.

A junior high school class in physical education learns the meaning of "football" in the United States and in Europe.

A junior high school assembly enjoys a program of Nigerian music
and dancing.

A junior high school class in homemaking compares life in North and
South America.

A senior high school class in world history compiles a list of Nobel
Prize winners in science.

A senior high school class in English reads from a list of novels about
life in Asia.

Generalization, essentially political in nature: "The recognition of
human rights and human dignity is basic to personal relationships and to
government."

A second grade class learns to settle a dispute, to analyze the cause
of the argument, and to arrive at a fair decision.

A fourth grade class learns to organize itself into a democratic group
and to elect officers.

A fifth grade class studies the United Nations Declaration of Human
Rights.

A sixth grade class compares the rights and responsibilities of a
citizen of the Soviet Union with those of a citizen of the United
States.

A junior high school social studies class compares the preamble of
the United States Constitution with the preamble of the United
Nations Charter.

A junior high school Pen Pal Club prepares an exhibit of postage
stamps.

A senior high school physical education class studies the effects of
the Cold War on the Olympic Games.

A senior high school World Affairs Club conducts a model session of
the United Nations Security Council and invites other schools to
participate.[20]

The Glens Falls Project is not a tightly organized effort to lock step the
social studies student through certain cross-cultural experiences; instead, all
teachers, not just social studies teachers, are encouraged to use any means at
their disposal to make their teaching more cross cultural. The lack of any
systematic scheme involving highly sophisticated research techniques to follow
teachers' innovative efforts is the basis for some criticism of the Glens Falls
Project.

A more highly organized effort to implement anthropological concepts

[20]Long and King, *op. cit.,* pp. 30-31.

may be found at the Edsel Ford High School, Dearborn, Michigan. The program originated in 1954 when a group of teachers attended the University of Chicago under a grant from the Ford Foundation. The two years at the University of Chicago were highlighted by meetings with Robert Redfield. The group was most impressed with Redfield's thesis that the study and analysis of a folk society is the best way to develop the ability to analyze and understand one's own society and its culture. The following organizing elements supported Redfield's thesis and still form the basis for the Dearborn experiment:

ORGANIZING ELEMENTS

Concepts
1. Every individual is born with basic drives he strives to satisfy within the framework of his culture.
2. The interaction of individuals and groups leads to the development of social institutions.
3. Social institutions tend to resist changes made necessary by technological advances, the rate of change is accelerated because of these technological advances but there is a proportionately greater lag in adjusting.
4. There is a constant interaction between man and his physical and cultural environment.

Values
1. Respect for the dignity and worth of the individual as a human dignity.
2. Appreciation of the contributions of individuals and groups for the improvement of mankind.
3. Appreciation of the democratic way of life with its rights and responsibilities.
4. Respect for truth and logic.
5. Appreciation for the contributions of other cultures to our culture.

Attitudes and Skills
1. In the techniques of locating, appraising and interpreting data.
2. In the techniques of group activities.
3. In thinking critically in areas of persistent social problems.

Interest
1. In contemporary problems.[21]

[21]Grace Kachaturoff, "Implementing Anthropological Concepts in the High School Curriculum," March 7, 1967 (mimeographed copy, in author's possession). The author is also indebted to Grace Kachaturoff, Chairman of the Social Studies Department at Edsel Ford High School, Dearborn, Michigan, for other materials related to the Dearborn project. These materials have been drawn upon freely in the discussion of the Dearborn project in this chapter.

The Edsel Ford social studies program is divided into three broad areas which consist of five semester-long required courses. The first semester of the sophomore year revolves around the general subject, culture, and consists of the study of selected folk societies. It is during this semester that the student learns basic anthropological concepts, such as customs, value systems, and cultural change. Moving from that which is simpler to that which is more complex, students study the Adaman Islanders, the Hopi Indians, and the Buganda of the British African colony of Uganda. Throughout their cultural analyses students are encouraged to find ways in which people in each culture seek to satisfy their basic drives. The next three semesters emphasize American society and culture. The first semester of the senior year is devoted to a study of persistent problems of our society.

Research conducted by Stanley Dimond of the University of Michigan compliments the Dearborn experiment for its systematic plan for analyzing the basic activities and institutions of human society and its special contribution to the evolution of social studies programs in our nation.

Comparative Approaches in Particular Social Studies Classes[22]

Although the comparative approach may not be the basis for the entire social studies curriculum, it may be used as the basis for an entire course such as world history. The comparative approach has probably been most frequently used at the secondary level in political science oriented classes. Comparative political systems and comparative political ideologies are the subject matter for some social studies classes, usually at the twelfth grade level. The course is often entitled "Problems of Democracy." A general theme of such courses is that there are x number of basic ideologies (for example, democracy, totalitarianism, and authoritarianism[23] or the totalitarian way of life and the democratic way of life[24]). The authors of the basic ideologies' thesis accentuate the differences rather than the similarities between ideologies. The reader-teacher and his students should certainly question whether or not these broad typologies are accurate and useful teaching categories.

[22]The excellent work done by the Anthropology Curriculum Study Project, 5632 Kimbark Avenue, Chicago, Illinois, is available to the reader. Malcolm Collier is the Director of this project. Other anthropologically oriented programs are: cultural anthropology at Francis W. Parker School in Chicago; the University of Chicago Laboratory School; Alexander Hamilton Junior High School in Seattle, Washington; and the Intercultural Education Project of the Palo Alto Unified School District, Palo Alto, California. The exclusion of these experimental programs in this chapter's discussion was due to a lack of space to treat each in a proper manner.

[23]John S. Gibson, *Ideology and World Affairs* (Boston: Houghton Mifflin Company, 1964).

[24]William Ebenstein, *Today's Isms* (Englewood Cliffs, N.J.: Prentice-Hall, Inc., 1964).

A somewhat different approach is prescribed in the Holt Social Studies Curriculum course dealing with Comparative Political Systems.[25] According to its authors, "Despite their differences, governments at all times and in all places have faced similar political problems. Social scientists call a one- or two-word statement of one of these problems a concept." The authors go on to say, "In this unit you will deal with five concepts which you will always find useful as tools to help you analyze governments:

1. Leadership: How does a political system recruit, train and assign tasks to political leaders?
2. Decision-making: How are political decisions made and carried out on the local, intermediate, and national levels in all branches of government?
3. Institutions: What political institutions does a society develop?
4. Ideology: Why does a society organize a particular type of government and how does it explain and justify its government?
5. The role of the citizen: What role does the individual citizen play in the government?"[26]

In the first unit of the Holt series, the students apply the five preceding concepts and questions to a World War II prisoner-of-war camp. This experimental unit is most imaginative and previews a well organized and exciting new series of social studies texts for secondary social studies teachers and students. The unit on "Government at Stoerpenberg Camp" is part of a ninth grade semester's course on Comparative Political Systems.

A second semester's course in the Holt Social Studies Curriculum series is entitled "Comparative Economic Systems." The course description reads as follows: "A Comparison of a traditional economy with systems where most decisions are made by the market (United States) and where most decisions are made by command (Soviet Union), focusing upon three basic questions—what is produced, how it is to be produced, and for whom it is to be produced.[27] Once again it can be seen that the course is built around organizing concepts and key questions.

In 1958 the Pennsylvania State Council of Education made a course, "World Cultures," mandatory for all students graduating from high school,

[25]The general editor of this series is Edwin Fenton, Historian at Carnegie Institute of Technology.
[26]Mindella Schultz and Howard Mehlinger, *Comparative Political Systems: An Inquiry Approach*, Edwin Fenton, ed. (New York: Holt, Rinehart & Winston, Inc., 1967), pp. 2-3.
[27]*Teacher's Guide for Three Experimental Units*, Edwin Fenton, ed. (New York: Holt, Rinehart & Winston, Inc., 1966), p. 13.

beginning in 1961.[28] The geographical approach to the study of cultures has been favored with a study of beliefs, customs, and characteristics of the peoples after the initial geographical approach. Suggested objectives for the course are listed below:

Suggested Objectives

Behavioral changes sought through the social sciences in the secondary school in our time suggest the inclusion of these purposes:

1. To reduce parochial or provincial attitudes of superiority or paternalism.
2. To become conscious of the continuum of mankind's ethical and intellectual development.
3. To become conscious of the interrelationships among different cultures in ethical and intellectual development throughout mankind's history.
4. To become conscious of philosophies, literatures, arts, and histories, other than our own, and to begin to learn from them.
5. To accept the idea that culture is not necessarily either good or bad—culture merely is.
6. To accept the idea that there is a reason for every strange thing in a foreign culture.
7. To become emotionally involved to the extent that figures, facts, and other abstractions begin to be interpreted in terms of human beings.
8. In short, to develop empathy.[29]

The following is an illustration of content of culture considered in one geographic section of Asia: The Indian Subcontinent.

An Illustration of Content of Culture in
Consideration of One Geographic Section of
Asia: The Indian Subcontinent

What are some areas of content vital to considering the cultures of one area, as an illustration? This illustration must of necessity be very brief and must be certainly less than complete and comprehensive. It cannot be organized into an outline for a model source unit. The purpose here is to suggest some aspects of culture vital to an initial understanding of the

[28] The book which describes this course of study is *The Study of World Cultures in Secondary Schools,* Report of a Conference Conducted by South Penn School Study Council and the Philadelphia Suburban School Study Council, Group B (Danville, Ill.: Interstate Printers & Publishers, Inc., 1962).

[29] *Ibid.,* pp. 67-68.

tremendous land mass so vital to the peace of the world—the Indian Subcontinent.

The Indian Subcontinent consists, roughly, of India, Pakistan, Nepal, and Ceylon. Divided naturally from the remainder of Asia and large enough to be a continent itself, it is often called a subcontinent. It is a huge land area with a huge population. It is an ancient area with history recorded far back into the days before Christ. Because of the need for brevity, and because it is obvious that they must be included, history and geography will only be mentioned. Attention will be focused on the nonhistorical aspects of cultures in this area.

The religions. A study of ethics in the holy books of Islam, Buddhism, and Hinduism will reveal explanations for many things and will illuminate the student's understanding of history. When the student understands even a little of Islam and Hinduism, he looks at the 1947 partition of India with new perception. He begins to understand why Ghandi was impressed by Thoreau, and is prepared to consider Muslims and Hindus as human beings who are ready to act upon the truth that "freedom is a hard-bought thing." The similarities between the Islamic ethic and the Judaeo-Christian ethic are startling to the young student and bring the Muslim much closer to him than he has ever been before. The differences between Muslims and Hindus in ethics and taboos bring a beginning of understanding of the implications of the disturbing mixture of geographic unity and ideological conflict in the Subcontinent.

The caste system. The caste system is interwoven so intricately into the total life of India that, despite efforts to eradicate it, its effects will remain with Hindus for generations and generations to come. There are hundreds of castes and subcastes, not just Brahmins and untouchables. Although not a caste system (since Islams abhor anything inimical to the equality of all men before God), the Muslims have practiced for many years, in the cases of some trades, the inherited occupation. With the caste system among the Hindus and inherited occupations among a large number of Muslims, countries find it almost impossible to develop a strong middle class, a fact with tremendous implications.

Colonialism, feudalism, and illiteracy. Until less than twenty years ago, the entire area, with the exception of Nepal, was a colonial part of the British Empire and had been colonial for many generations. What does such a fact do to people? Initiative necessary to self-government and to resourcefulness in village and town could not develop. The education system followed the line laid down in the early nineteenth century by Macaulay—educated colored "Englishmen" to serve under white Englishmen. Cooperative discussion, cooperative resourcefulness, cooperative responsibility—none of these could begin to develop until only a very few years ago.

Feudalism, despite the break-up of the separate princely states at the time of partition, still exists. As late as 1958 a decree was issued in Pakistan to take away the huge landholdings of landlords and to allow peasants who had been held in fief for many decades to buy their own lands.

Literacy in their own languages is possessed by perhaps fewer than one-fifth of the people. The germ theory of disease is widely unknown. Epidemics of cholera and smallpox come with horrible regularity, and if one asks about the illness of a dying child, he is nearly always told that the child has a fever—that is all that is known.

Languages. In the Indian Subcontinent, there are at least 225 main languages and dialects. Each of these is precious to some people. Rioting among language groups in Ceylon has been reported for years, and language is one of the sore points with which government must contend in both India and Ceylon. The language of education at the college and university level is English, often the only language in which two gentlemen from different parts of India can converse with understanding of each other. Language is very close to the hearts of human beings and it has all sorts of ramifications in the characteristics of the person.

Literature. Not all the languages have produced substantial bodies of literature, but at least three writers, all represented in English by good translations, come to mind immediately: Sir Mohammad Iqbal, Sir Rabindranath Tagore, and Sarojini Naidu. Sarojini Naidu wrote delicate, lovely lyrics worthy of places with the early work of Edna St. Vincent Millay, and closed her career as a high political official in West Bangal after the 1947 partition of India. Iqbal was as much a philosopher as poet, and he laid the philosophic base for the creation of a single land for Muslims of the Subcontinent, Pakistan. His poetry is of high quality, and much of it weighty. Tagore, probably the best known because he was a recipient of the Nobel Prize for Literature, wrote in Bangali, and every Bangali-speaker knows Tagore. His poetry is recited at every opportunity, and his dance-dramas are presented very frequently. In the poems and dramas, heavy with symbolism, can be found many of the values of India. One of the dance-dramas, *The King of the Dark Chamber,* had a run of about eight months in an off-Broadway theatre in New York in 1961.

Also there must be mentioned the large amount of literature of the west which deals with the Indian Subcontinent. There is hardly any more exciting introduction to the mutiny of the Indians against the British, in 1857, than John Masters' novel *Nightrunners of Bengal.* This is as rousing a novel of adventure as has appeared in a long time, and it presents authentic history in terms of fully-drawn human beings. Many of Masters' novels are historical and present authentically much of the culture: *The Deceivers; The Lotus and the Wind; Bhowani Junction; Far, Far the Mountain Peak; Coromandel!; The Venus of Konpara;* and the autobiographical book, *Bugles and a Tiger.*

One cannot list here many writers, but bibliographies are available. But surely there is time to mention *the* novel of India in English: E. M. Forster's *A Passage to India,* which does a thoroughly accurate and artistic job of setting the values. of Indians against the values of Englishmen; Kamala Markandaya's tragic and poignant novel of village life in India, *Nectar in a Sieve;* a recent book of autobiographical sketches by Santha Rama Rau, called *Gifts of Passage;* and that book of living human beings by Margaret Parton, *The Leaf and the Flame.* Lest they be forgotten, we must mention particularly the ancient books of ethics, values, and religion. Among those are the *Bhagavad Gita,* the *Ramayana,* and the *Quran.*

The arts. Music, painting, and other arts (including literature, already mentioned) are highly esteemed by the people. The famous paintings on the adventurous rock mountain in Ceylon, Sigiriya, date back to the fifth century. The caves at Ajanta and Elephanta have attracted artistic interest for many years, with their painting and sculpture, all very old. Hindu temples abound with strange and interesting sculpture, nearly all related closely to the beliefs and rituals connected with the religion.

Today the artist in the Indian Subcontinent still occupies a place of high standing. So interested are the Pakistanis that, even with their very poor economy, they provide scholarships for young people, no matter from what social class they may come, who are talented in art. The poet is a respected man, and so is the painter. In these cultures there is no suggestion of effeminacy in such activities, as there is in middleclass American culture.

Sources of civilization. Recent excavations have disclosed cities indicating a flourishing civilization of some advancement dating back to at least 3000 B.C. Three of these excavated cities, of which most are in the Indus River Valley in West Pakistan, are Mohen-Jo-Daro, Taxila, and Harappa.

Miscellaneous. The government in each of the Subcontinent's nations is not a duplicate of the United States form of representative democracy. Yet democracy, in its forms of adaptation, is beginning to grow strong in all the countries. Even in Pakistan, where the man who is now President took control by force in 1958, there is the first hope of democracy since almost the birth of the country in 1947; yet the form of government bears little outward resemblance to our own.

Materialism has little standing in the values of these people. Resources of importance are inner resources of the spirit. Persons are judged most often by their actions and inferred ethics. Wealth and poverty are factors that make little difference in the judgment of a man's basic qualities.

The machine-made article is rare; the hand-made article is commonplace. Millions exist on a bare subsistence level. Not yet has elementary education become compulsory. The systems of education are characterized by incredibly large drop-out rates and large percentages of failures; the school is only now beginning to be looked upon as something related to better life in the community as well as preparation for professional or clerical careers.

Nothing, or almost nothing, has been said about economics, sanitation, geography, racial differences, philosophies, architecture, music, dance, social etiquette, and many other aspects of the culture. As we intended, nothing was said of history. The history of the Subcontinent is filled with violence, vanquishings of whole peoples, the rise to prominence of powerful men of whom some were truly great. For centuries, the west has depended upon the Indian Subcontinent for much in material things. Now, it still depends upon it for a multitude of reasons, most of them tied in with the survival of the free world.

Only some of the aspects of cultures in the Subcontinent have been indicated. Our goal is identification with the individuals who make up these nations, so that they may be looked upon as human beings. The reaching of the goals which we have set for teaching this area of nonwestern cultures will be enhanced by using human beings and their needs, ethics, values, customs, and difficulties in bringing to life the history and geography of the area.

What is immediately and easily available for teachers and for students to use in studying this geographic area, the Indian Subcontinent, and other nonwestern areas? There are many books—a great many in inexpensive paperbound editions— on many subjects, including history, religions, art, philosophies, and literature. The amount of materials designed specifically for teaching about Asia and Africa in secondary schools has increased very, very rapidly from almost nothing six or eight years ago.

A few novels in English about the Subcontinent have already been listed. Many pieces of literature other than novels are also available. Much of the music of the cultures mentioned has been recorded and is available on long-playing discs.

Metropolitan sections of the United States have within them at any one time hundreds of natives of nonwestern lands, many of them graduate students. There is an even larger number of Americans who have lived and worked there.

Various organizations have collections of pictures for exhibit and use. Nearly every college and university of any size has at least one professor who is a specialist in some aspect of Asia. Libraries dealing only with certain world areas exist at some colleges and universities. Large public libraries maintain good collections of books concerned with many aspects of cultures in the Subcontinent and other areas.

Embassies of the countries will supply useful materials. Both the embassies and the United Nations, with citizens who have knowledge of these countries, are interested in helping.[30]

Comparative Approaches in Social Studies Units

Some social studies teachers may not wish to employ comparative approaches for any great length of time but instead want to adopt a comparative approach to a unit of six weeks or less. One way to achieve this is to use abbreviated forms of comparative approaches which ordinarily are employed for a full course. For example, the Holt materials on comparative political systems may be tacked on to a course in "Problems of Democracy" thereby covering the last six weeks of the senior year. However, in each case where the teacher wants to adopt the more eclectic unit approach, he will probably find it most satisfactory to build his own teaching unit. The following is an example of such a unit based on the use of comparisons. The group involved consisted of twelfth grade students in a government and economics course. The students would have to be described as above average suburbanites, most of whom planned to go on for higher education.

Previous to the final comparative unit the students have read a variety of paperbacks from Plato's *Republic* to D. W. Brogan's *The American Character*. The two main books assigned during the final six weeks were *Communism*, by Alfred G. Meyer and *Freedom and Responsibility and the American Way of Life*, by Carl Becker. The basic comparison to be made was between the Soviet Union's brand of communism and the United States political system. Particular attention was paid to foreign policies of the respective countries with George Kennan's book, *American Diplomacy*, used as a source book. Two evening seminars were held during the six week period: at the first seminar Alfred G. Meyer answered a barrage of questions about his controversial comparative thesis; at the second seminar Wesley Fishel discussed United States foreign policy in general and Vietnam and Laos in particular.

Meyer's controversial comparative thesis was the main subject of contention during the entire six week period. According to Meyer, the most significant event in any country's history is its industrial revolution and the related growth of bureaucracies. As a political sociologist Meyer proceeds to

[30] *Ibid.*, pp. 75-80.

compare Stalin with Henry Ford and Khrushchev with Henry Ford II. He also compares Soviet youth organizations, such as the Komsomol, with United States youth organizations, such as fraternities and sororities. Life in the Soviet Union under Stalin is also compared to life on military complexes belonging to the United States. What is the value of such comparisons? According to Meyer,

> Comparisons are useful in several ways. For one thing, political science may make significant advances by comparing and classifying phenomena in different systems and fitting these into broad typologies. Second, comparison is a useful didactic device, because we understand the unfamiliar much more easily when it is presented in terms of the familiar. Conversely, we may gain better understanding even of the familiar by seeing it reflected in the warped mirror of unfamiliar but related phenomena.[31]

One student posed the following questions to Professor Meyer: "What if the two systems being compared have more differences than similarities? Isn't the comparison then more misleading than it is useful?" These questions are indicative of the interest generated by the use of comparisons and the related further study which accompanied such interest. The use of comparisons had indeed proved to be a useful teaching and learning device.

The Occasional Use of Comparisons

The fourth use of comparisons is probably most commonly employed in social studies classes. Instead of being used on a systematic basis, comparisons are spontaneously made at the discretion of the teacher and his students. Analogies are frequently used to bolster one's argument; for example, "you know what happened to the press in Nazi Germany; if we aren't careful. . . ." Analogies are also used to make seemingly "dead" areas of the past come to life; for example, "the French Revolution can best be understood if we look at the Watts Riots."

It is, however, possible to be more rigorous with one's comparisons even though they are made on an occasional basis.

> I am reminded of a problem with a slow learner class I once had, which made a comparison of the ethics of the Buddhist precepts and the Hebrew ideas of the Ten Commandments. These children, who were extremely poor readers and had a very difficult time grasping a lot of things, began to see, for example, that the Ten Commandments are expressed in a negative tone. The Buddhist precepts are expressed in a much more positive tone, and they began to question why this was the case.[32]

[31] Alfred G. Meyer, *The Soviet Political System* (New York: Random House, Inc., 1965), p. 10.
[32] William Hering, Jr., "Concepts, Processes and Values," *Concepts and Structure in the*

Cross-cultural comparisons are perhaps the most obvious to the reader; for example, compare the United States and the Soviet Union in the early 1930's as to their systems of economic arrangements. However, comparisons may also be made within a particular system; for example, compare the system of economic arrangements which the United States had in the early 1930's to the system which we have today.

Finally, let it be said that the effective teacher should have his students honestly evaluate the use of comparisons and build cases for their positions on this matter.

Advantages in Using the Comparative Approach

It is often difficult to begin studying a new area. For example, the teacher might ask himself, "How am I going to introduce this unit on the Soviet Union so that enough interest will be generated to stimulate further inquiry?" In this case, the comparative approach may prove to be a useful heuristic device in introducing an area of study. The teacher may simply say, "I'm interested in your ideas as to how people in the United States and the Soviet Union are alike and different from each other." Or he may say, "What are people in the Soviet Union like?" After getting a response, the teacher may then have the students compare characteristics of Soviet citizens with those of citizens of the United States.

Admittedly, many gross generalizations will be tendered by social studies students. The important thing at this point is that interest in the subject has been stimulated and hypotheses have been generated. In the process the comparative approach may act as a sorting device.

It is now up to the teacher and his students to systematically explore the hypotheses made when the comparative approach was first used. In the course of this exploration comparisons may continue to be made and hypotheses refined. It now becomes evident that the comparative approach is valuable not only in acquiring information but in facilitating interest in inquiry as the student continues to explore a new field of study.

The comparative approach may also be used as a very sophisticated approach after an individual has a deep understanding of the several subjects being compared. Therefore, comparisons between the Soviet Union, the United States, and Great Britain may be made by D.W. Brogan or the ninth grade social studies student. This in fact is the main advantage of the approach; it is useful to the inquirer at any stage of his intellectual development.

It is quite possible for the social studies student, for example in World

---

New Social Science Curricula (West Lafayette, Ind.: Social Science Education Consortium, Inc., 1966), p. 45.

History, to get lost amidst the flood of details. The comparative approach may be useful in giving the student perspective as to the overall "style" of one group, society, or culture compared to other comparable units.

Another way the comparative approach may be used to advantage is in relating events to a common theme in several countries. For example, the desire of underdeveloped countries to industrialize may be examined in a study of two or more underdeveloped countries. It is also possible to compare and contrast forces which seek to maintain the status quo (tradition) and forces seeking social change through modernization; this comparison may be made in a single country or it may be examined cross culturally. In fact, one of the most profitable uses of the comparative approach is as a kind of interaction analysis of the dynamics of social change.

Those who use the cross-cultural approach hope their students will become less ethnocentric and more world-minded. Whether or not this admirable objective is achieved should be the subject of more research by those interested in social studies education.

The comparative approach is not an end in itself but is directed toward a more comprehensive objective—understanding. As a didactic device the comparative approach should help us ". . .understand the unfamiliar much more easily when it is presented in terms of the familiar." It is also true that ". . .we may gain better understanding even of the familiar by seeing it reflected in the warped mirror of unfamiliar but related phenomena."[33]

It should be reiterated that the previous discussion deals with the comparative approach as a teaching device for secondary social studies; a discussion of the comparative approach as a basis for research at the university level has deliberately been omitted.

Problems in Using the Comparative Approach

It should be obvious to the reader that the comparative approach may be used for any end. It is possible to use this approach to study a religion or several religions; it is also possible to promote *a* religion by using the comparative approach. The teacher and class must work together to establish criteria for classification. Furthermore, all areas must be open for investigation and a variety of sources must be used rather than a single textbook with predetermined answers. In short, a classroom atmosphere of inquiry must be created whereby *the teacher* and *the students* are able to investigate any hypothesis.

The whole classroom situation becomes more complex if one adopts the comparative approach. The inquiry approach takes precedence over right or wrong answers. Objectives, procedures to reach objectives, and evaluation

[33] Meyer, *op. cit.,* p. 10.

measures must relate to inquiry as a process of learning. Understandings achieved by using comparisons are proximate, not definitive, and are therefore open to further inquiry. If those wishing to adopt the comparative approach hope to discover absolute laws, they will most likely be disappointed.

Some contend that the comparative approach is superficial and particular studies are more intellectually honest. In the author's opinion, the advantages in stimulating students to inquire outweigh the previously mentioned criticism. Such criticism would seem to be more valid when applied to the use of the comparative approach in university research. However, at the secondary school level it is most important to interest students in subject areas in which they are too often bored. Whether or not the comparative approach is less intellectually honest than the traditional or newly prescribed alternative approaches must be researched in a variety of situations. At present we rely more on hunches than empirical data in answering such questions.

In using the comparative approach, the teacher and his students may tend to overemphasize differences at the expense of similarities which exist in order to provoke further inquiry. Differences appear to be more intriguing and invite explanation. The result is to present a distorted view of particular subjects being compared.[34]

The comparative approach may also become a game which is played at the expense of more effective ways of learning. Games are time-consuming and there is plenty of classroom time to consume in secondary schools. Until more sophisticated research findings are available, the teacher must use trial and error to see if the use of the comparative approach is effective in various learning situations.

In conclusion, it must be said that the user of the comparative approach should be aware of its limitations and always be ready to dig deeper to test his tentative conclusions. For example, the student has been to a baseball game in the United States and notes that whistling usually indicates support of a player or team. The student has also heard from his uncle, who has visited Spain recently, that whistling occurs at bullfights. The overt act of whistling is the same in both situations; however, the student must seek more information in order to realize that whistling at a bullfight in Spain indicates disapproval. The same overt act has two different meanings in different cultures.

Annotated Bibliography

Andreski, Stanislav, *Elements of Comparative Sociology.* Weidenfield and Nicolson, London, 1964. Bothered by what he considers the neglect of the

---

[34] The American habit of policy making by analogy is criticized by Senator J. William Fulbright: ". . .North Vietnam's involvement in South Vietnam, for example, is equated with Hitler's invasion of Poland and a parley with the Viet Cong would represent 'another

comparative method in modern sociology, the author focuses on the methodology, substantive general problems, and case studies involved in the use of the comparative method in sociology. Part One, Chapters 1-6 should be of special interest to the reader.

Borton, Hugh, *et. al., The College and World Affairs.* Report on the Committee on the College and World Affairs, New York, 1964. Chapter III, "Developing the Educational Program" discusses existing university programs employing the cross-cultural approach. The need for more programs employing the comparative approach is clearly spelled out for the reader.

Brown, John W., Cashin, H. John, Kovinick, Philip, and Grether, Richard, *Contemporary International Problems.* Centinela Valley Union High School District, Hawthorne, California, 1962. This interesting book was prepared by high school teachers of comparative government, economics, and world affairs. Unit IV, Modern Nations: A Political, Economic, and Cultural Comparison, should be a special interest to the reader.

Brubaker, Dale L., "A Comparative Cultures Approach to the Teaching of Vocational and Citizenship Education in Secondary Schools." Unpublished doctoral dissertation, Michigan State University, East Lansing, Michigan, 1965. This is a study of the practical application of the comparative cultures approach in a secondary school classroom situation. The classes involved were ninth grade classes in civics and vocational guidance. Students were randomly assigned to two experimental classes and two control classes. Overall results demonstrated little change in either experimental or control groups on the basis of research instruments used.

Chandler, Alfred D. Jr., *Strategy and Structure.* The Massachusetts Institute of Technology Press, Cambridge, Mass., 1962. Chapter 6, "Organizational Innovation–A Comparative Analysis," should be of special interest to the reader. Professor Chandler has conducted a comparative analysis of organizational innovation in four major corporations (du Pont, General Motors, Jersey Standard, and Sears). During the 1920's these corporations adopted a "decentralized," multidivisional structure. Chandler's comparative business history is aimed at providing ". . .deeper probes into the nature of the function studied, and so provide more accurate interpretations and more meaningful evaluations of the performances of several different enterprises in that activity than could a whole series of histories of individual firms."

Munich.' The treatment of slight and superficial resemblances as if they were full-blooded analogies–as instances, as it were, of history 'repeating itself'–is a substitute for thinking and a misuse of history." J. William Fulbright, *The Arrogance of Power* (New York: Vintage Books, 1966), pp. 31-32.

[Introduction, p. 1.] The advantage of Chandler's use of the comparative method is that "...it makes it possible to relate these detailed analyses more clearly and more precisely to broader historical developments." [Introduction, p. 7.]

Ebenstein, William, *Today's ISMS.* Prentice-Hall, Inc., Englewood Cliffs, N.J., 1964. Employing the way of life concept rather than one particular aspect, such as government or economics, Professor Ebenstein compares the totalitarian way of life and the democratic way of life: in the former he includes totalitarian communism and totalitarian fascism; in the latter he includes democratic capitalism and democratic socialism. The author sees these two ways of life as diametrically opposed thereby accentuating the differences rather than similarities between them.

Evans-Pritchard, E.E., *The Comparative Method in Social Anthropology.* L.T. Hobhouse Memorial Trust Lecture, No. 33, Delivered on 14 May 1963 at The London School of Economics and Political Science, London. The Athlone Press, London, 1963. It is interesting to compare this short work with Whiting's article. Both deal with the history of the use of the comparative method but Evans-Pritchard's non-American background in the use of the comparative method makes his work most interesting.

Gallagher, James, *An Annotated Bibliography of Anthropological Materials for High Schools Use.* The Macmillan Company, New York, 1967. Approximately 350 books annotated. Sponsored by the Anthropology Curriculum Study Project.

Gibson, John S., *Ideology and World Affairs.* Houghton Mifflin Company, Boston, 1964. This book is sponsored by The Lincoln Filene Center for Citizenship and Public Affairs under the general editorship of Franklin Patterson. Dr. Gibson first developed this book's contents in a series of fifteen television programs. The author contends that there are three basic ideologies: democracy, totalitarianism, and authoritarianism. Emphasis is placed on the differences between these three ideologies. These ideologies are then related to world affairs as the title of this book indicates.

Kardiner, Abram, with the collaboration of Ralph Linton, Cora Du Bois, and James West, *The Psychological Frontiers of Society.* Columbia University Press, New York, 1946. This is a collaborative work by an anthropologist, Ralph Linton, and a psychologist, Abram Kardiner. The concept of basic personality types refers to "...the value-attitude systems which are basic to the individual's personality configuration." [Foreword, p. viii.] Two main questions were posed: How were these basic personality types produced? and

What influence did they exert on the culture itself? Cross-cultural analyses are undertaken by the authors to answer these questions.

Lasswell, Harold, *Politics.* McGraw-Hill Book Company, 1936. This book presents concepts and gives an analysis of a study of the influence and the influential in political behavior. The comparative method is used throughout the book to explain the distribution of deference, i.e., Roman Catholic hierarchy. The structure of the Soviet Union and the United States governments are discussed in reference to the concept that very few will make it to the top (elite group).

Long, Harold M., and King, Robert N., *Improving the Teaching of World Affairs,* National Council for the Social Studies Bulletin Number 35, Washington, D.C., 1964. This is the story of the Glens Falls School System and its attempts to make teachers, students, and the community more international minded.

Meyer, Alfred G., *The Soviet Political System.* Random House, Inc., New York, 1965. Especially see the Introduction for a discussion of Professor Meyer's use of the comparative method. The author uses the comparative method as a didactic device.

Moore, F. W. (ed.), *Readings in Cross-Cultural Methodology.* Human Relations Area Files Press, New York, 1966. This is a compilation of articles dealing with the comparative method. It is the most comprehensive single book on the comparative method and its use in social anthropology.

Service, E.R., *Profiles in Ethnology.* Harper & Row, Publishers, New York, 1963. The preface is a good account of the bases of cultural levels of organization. Ethnologies of twenty-one cultures around the world are given from the Arunta of Australia (band level) to a modern communist Chinese Peasant Village (modern folk societies). Use for any social studies course where cultural emphasis is needed.

Shibutani, Tamotsu, and Kwan, Kian M., *Ethnic Stratification.* The Macmillan Company, New York, 1965. The authors have attempted to sketch the outlines of a comprehensive theory of inter-ethnic contacts, a set of generalizations that enable us to look at diverse and seemingly unrelated episodes as manifestations of the same recurrent processes.

The Study of World Cultures in Secondary Schools. Report of a Conference Conducted by South Penn Study Council and the Philadelphia Suburban School Study Council, Group B, The Interstate Printers & Publishers, Inc.,

Danville, Ill., 1962. In 1958 a "World Cultures" course was made mandatory in Pennsylvania for those students graduating from high school, beginning in 1961. This report is from a work conference on the world cultures course.

Whiting, John W. M., "The Cross-Cultural Method," *Handbook of Social Psychology,* Vol. I. Addison-Wesley Publishing Co., Inc., Reading, Massachusetts, 1954. Professor Whiting's article is probably the most definitive single article on the cross-cultural method. There is an excellent discussion of the history of the use of the cross-cultural method.

CHAPTER 8

The Study of National Character

Dale L. Brubaker

Introduction

The social studies curriculum has traditionally been the stronghold for the teaching of history; yet, it would not be completely fair or accurate to say that advocates of history have simply fortified themselves from the intrusions of others, particularly the behavioral scientists. The others in this case excluded themselves by default. As a result, narrative history—with its flair for the dramatic—has been the particular brand of history taught in social studies classes in the United States. Despite Carl Becker's dictum that every man should be his own historian, historiography has been reserved for graduate students with undergraduates largely confined to survey courses. Likewise, few instances of historical analysis and the writing of history in social studies classes have been reported. Authors of social studies textbooks, usually educationists and public school administrators, have too often provided social studies students with a smorgasbord of meaningless, if not also academically questionable, facts and incidents. One American history textbook goes so far as to have an American flag atop the flagship of Columbus. It is interesting to speculate as to what Columbus would have thought of this, let alone Queen Isabella.

Recent efforts to streamline the social studies curriculum have reflected the possible value of the behavioral sciences; a concomitant criticism of history has occurred, though critics often fail to make a distinction between history as it was taught and history as it could or should have been taught. At any rate, history is expected to go modern in the social studies curriculum; part of this modernity depends on historians employing the findings and methods of inquiry used by behavioral scientists. For this reason, one of the most admired contemporary historians in some social studies circles is David M. Potter.

Professor Potter's book, *People of Plenty,* is often cited by innovative social studies educators, such as Byron G. Massialas and C. Benjamin Cox, as an example of a work by an historian who has drawn ideas from the behavioral sciences, thus successfully updating the teaching of history. *People of Plenty* includes an interdisciplinary study of national character in general, plus a specific tracing of a particular theme, American abundance and its role in the forming of the American character. Not only have Potter's efforts been commended for their value at the university level, but they have also been prescribed as a kind of prototype for social studies innovation.

The writings of David M. Potter and Alfred D. Chandler, Jr., and coursework with D. W. Brogan prompted the writer of this chapter to explore the interesting possibilities of the study of national character for social studies students. Such explorations took the form of experimental studies with twelfth grade students in government and economics classes. The writings of Massialas and Cox added fuel to the fire, and this chapter is the result of efforts to integrate many loosely defined ideas previously held. It is the thesis of Massialas and Cox that the social studies curriculum should be organized around generalizations or concepts not confined to a particular academic discipline.

This means, in effect, that their efforts are interdisciplinary rather than multidisciplinary; they feel, in fact, that the salvation of the social studies rests with the interdisciplinary approach being applied to important social issues.[1]

This chapter is, then, an attempt to explore the possibilities of using the concept of national character as an organizing concept or generalization in social studies classes. The advantages of using this conceptual approach are many; however, the main advantage, in the writer's opinion, is that the social sciences, especially the behavioral sciences, are drawn upon while at the same time giving history an important role in illuminating a nation's character. Efforts by some of our brightest historians to achieve such a synthesis demonstrate that social studies students may effect a similar, although less sophisticated, alliance.

The intent of this chapter is not simply to prescribe a theoretical model, important though that enterprise may be. The writer will also report the efforts of his former social studies students in using the concept of national character as an organizing device. This experience in turn prompted the writer to examine many other possible uses for the concept of national character, some of which will be discussed in the chapter.

---

[1] *Social Studies in the United States: A Critical Appraisal,* C. Benjamin Cox and Byron G. Massialas, eds. (New York: Harcourt, Brace & World, Inc., 1967), pp. 334-338.

The chapter begins with a brief history of the concept of national character and is brought to a close with a discussion of the advantages and problems associated with the use of national character as a concept to be employed in the social studies curriculum.

A Brief History of The Concept of National Character [2]

The concept of national character is not a recent phenomenon; the earliest formal discussion of the subject occurred in the fifth century before Christ in the writings of Hippocrates, a Greek physician. He saw the Asiatics as feeble, gentle, and less warlike than the Europeans mainly as a result of their less authoritarian institutions. "It seems valid to regard Hippocrates as the first writer on the subject of national character," writes David M. Potter, "because he approached it consciously as a problem of generalization about groups of people, while other writers did not do this."[3] Aristotle, unlike Hippocrates, had a static conception of national character emphasizing his belief that permanent climatic conditions caused changeless character traits.

Until recently, the concept of national character has been most frequently used by historians. It is also true that until recently attempts to explain national character have rested on three main argumentative bases: (1) the supernatural argument that a country consists of God's chosen people; (2) the belief that one's environment determines all, at the expense of man-made conditions; and (3) modern nationalism which emphasizes national virtues.[4]

As might be expected, historians have given a variety of meanings to the concept of national character; in fact, it is their failure to give a tight, precise definition which has allowed critics to cite the contradictions inherent in such definitions. Many scholars feel, however, that there are certain salient traits which commentators have attributed to the American in every period of this history. Examples are the belief in democracy, practicality, and prosperity.[5] The question of whether or not this is the case is worthy of investigation by social studies teachers and their students.

[2] The writer is indebted to David M. Potter, H.C.J. Duijker, and N.H. Frijda for their excellent writings on the history of the concept of national character. See: David M. Potter, *People of Plenty* (Chicago: University of Chicago Press, 1966), pp. 3-72; and H.C.J. Duijker and N.H. Frijda, *National Character and National Stereotypes* (Amsterdam, The Netherlands: North-Holland Publishing Co., 1960), pp. 1-49.

[3] Potter, *op. cit.*, p. 4.

[4] Potter, *op. cit.*, pp. 21-28.

[5] Max Lerner, *America as a Civilization*, vol. I (New York: Simon and Schuster, Inc., 1961), p. 67. A similar case is made by Henry Steele Commager as he advocates searching for the permanent rather than the transient in the American character, recurring themes and persistent traits rather than the fleeting. *America in Perspective*, Henry Steele Commager, ed. (New York: The New American Library of World Literature, Inc., 1961), pp.x-xi.

Although many contemporary historians still use the concept of national character in their writings, the behavioral scientists have done the most sophisticated work with the concept. In fact, David M. Potter goes so far as to say that " . . .the study of national character is today in the custody of the behavioral scientists and . . .they have earned their primacy in this field."[6]

It becomes obvious that the ultimate problem in using the concept of national character is a classificatory one: Is the classification imputed valid? That is, do nations, a term which is predominantly political, have a character?[7] Do people who are banded together politically have characteristics in common because of their political affiliation? Are there other stereotypes which are more valid and useful than those which occur because of political boundaries? At different stages of their development, nations are more nation conscious. Does this mean that they have more national character at these times? Can the concept of national character be broad enough to include the attitudes of a nation's inhabitants, a psychological matter, and their behavior, for example, as expressed in their cultural products? It can be easily seen that the concept of national character raises a whole myriad of questions, which in turn explains its usefulness as a heuristic device for the learner.

Many behavioral scientists prefer to deal with the concept "culture" rather than the concept "nation." How are culture and nation related and what does this relationship mean to our discussion of national character? As stated by Professor Potter, " . . .the character of a culture may become, or at least coincide with, the character of a nation, because the culture tends to realize itself politically through the process of national unification."[8]

The use of psychological and anthropological methods in studying national character had its origin in the United States during the World War II. Psychological warfare was but part of the waging of total war against little known and inaccessible enemies.[9] Developments have followed two major avenues of inquiry: cultural anthropology and child development along Freudian lines. Recent efforts have tried to combine these two lines of study into the general area of personality and culture with the recognition that they are always related to each other. Specific developments in the area of personality and culture are treated at length in several writings, but are somewhat involved and extraneous to this brief history of the concept of national character.[10]

---

[6]Potter, op. cit., p. 46.

[7]For a discussion of the lack of sophisticated research models dealing with modern national states and a proposal for such studies, see Alex Inkeles, "National Character and Modern Political Systems," in Francis L.K. Hsu ed., Psychological Anthropology (Homewood, Ill.: Dorsey Press, 1961), pp. 172-208.

[8]Potter, op. cit., p. 14.

[9]Margaret Mead, "The Study of National Character," in Daniel Lerner and Harold D. Lasswell eds., The Policy Sciences: Recent Developments in Scope and Method (Stanford, Calif.: Stanford University Press, 1951), p. 70.

[10]The best account, in the writer's opinion, may be found in ibid., pp. 77-85.

Employing the Concept of National Character in Social Studies Classes

The thesis of this chapter simply stated is that *the concept of national character may be a useful heuristic device for social studies teachers and students*. It is not contended that social studies students should be turned into sophisticated behavioral science research scholars. It is, however, the writer's belief, based on his own teaching experience in secondary schools, that the concept of national character may be useful in generating hypotheses which may be explored through dialogue, reading, and, in some cases, rather basic research procedures. Such an enterprise should not only foster inquiry, which, in the opinion of the writer, is the *raison d'etre* for the area of social studies, but it should also provoke the interest of students—an unfamiliar provocation to be sure in many, if not most, social studies classes.

These prescriptions on the part of the writer need to be supported in some practical way: a description of particular efforts to use the concept of national character in social studies classes may be of value to the reader. These efforts will probably appear to be crude. The teacher—innovator, however, was in his second year of teaching and initiated this approach without benefit of experimental curriculum guides or university consultants.

The following dialogue occurred in a twelfth grade class in government and economics. The academic year was divided into six six-week sessions; the ensuing description is but one week of the final six-week session.

Introduction to the study of the "American character" by the teacher:

Last year you studied American history. This year we have asked and tried to answer the following questions: Who should rule, or, stated another way, what system of power arrangements do you feel should exist in governing a nation? What kind of economic and political arrangements do we have in the United States today? How has this arrangement evolved to its present state? How do those who have economic and political power secure, perpetuate, and justify this power to themselves and others? How do elements of the population in the United States relate to those with economic and political power? This means that we have really dealt with description (that which is the case) and prescription (that which you feel should be the case).

We have read the following books in the process: The Republic (excerpts), by Plato; *The Prince,* by Machiavelli; *The "Higher Law" Background of American Constitutional Law,* by E. S. Corwin; *"Politics and the Human Covenant",* by John F. A. Taylor; *Foundations of American Constitutionalism,* by Andrew McLaughlin; *Second Treatise of Government,* by John Locke; *Letters from an American Farmer* (excerpts), by Crevecoeur; Charles Dickens' *American Notes;* and excerpts from your standard American Government text.

In the next six weeks you will read *The American Character,* by D. W. Brogan, *American Capitalism,* by Louis Hacker, and *The United States Political System and How It Works,* by David C. Coyle.

The general subject of this six week session is "The American Character: Does it really exist?"

Teacher: We have a number of foreign students in our school each year. One of our class members, Harri, has come from Sweden. If someone were to say to you, Harri, "What is an American?", what would you say?

Harri: I'm not sure.

Teacher: Let me rephrase my question: What were your first impressions of the United States?

Harri: Hamburgs, large grocery stores, and department stores, and great distances between different parts of the country. The students I first met also didn't seem to have much respect for their elders. They were more open.

Teacher: Harri has listed some characteristics he feels are typical of America and Americans. Can some of the rest of you add to his list?

A very rough list is compiled although there is some disagreement as to particular characteristics.

Student: It seems to me that we're on the wrong track. By this I mean that all men have certain desires such as a search for beauty, the need for food and clothing, and a desire to communicate. These common needs are felt by all men regardless of where they live, in Russia, the United States, France, Canada, etc.

Teacher: What can we call your argument? That is, what are you really saying about man?

Student: She's really saying that man has a nature. This is something I learned when I was a kid.

Teacher: Where did you learn this? Can you remember?

Student: In church I think. I learned that man is basically bad but can be made better through religion.

Another Student: But that's just one point of view. For example, when we read about Ben Franklin and discussed deism we saw that man was considered basically good.

Teacher: Good point. However, the thing these different interpretations have in common is that man was thought to have a basic nature. In other words, we might call this argument the "nature of man" argument.

Teacher: What does all of this have to do with national character?

Student: Well, if we say there is such a thing as the nature of man then there is no such thing as national character.

Another Student I disagree! There can be such a thing as the nature of man but still there are obvious differences in people in different countries.

Teacher: Anyone else like to add anything to this? How can we resolve this?

Student: You can say there is such a thing as the nature of man but this nature is expressed in different ways in different countries. I mean, for example, all men have a need for shelter but national characteristics, such as the climate, determine what kind of shelter is needed.

Teacher: Can you think of any other examples?

Student: I still think there is such a thing as the nature of man and therefore men are basically alike and therefore there is no such a thing as national character.

Teacher: It looks like we aren't going to resolve this today but you can now understand the "nature of man" argument and how it can be used to argue against the idea of national character. We'll come back to this argument and when you write your paper you can defend the point of view which you support.

Tomorrow you'll have time in class to read the books assigned. As usual, because of the large amount of reading assigned, you may read in class two days a week. This week we'll read on Tuesday and Thursday. I'll be glad to talk with you about any questions you have on your reading.

Second Discussion Session

Teacher: On Monday we listed what you considered to be characteristics of America and Americans. Yesterday you read part of Brogan's book, *The American Character*. Let's return to the list and see if you want to make any additions, subtractions, or raise any questions. In the process we'll try to ask the question, is there such a thing as the American character?

Student: I think there may be a difference between the characteristics of America and the characteristics of an American.

Teacher: What do you mean exactly?

Student: Well, Harri said that great distances exist between different parts of the United States but a student raised in New York City may not agree but instead say that the United States is very crowded. In other words, different Americans list different characteristics.

Another Student: That's true. We talked about this yesterday in the cafeteria. We argued all lunch period over some of the characteristics of Americans.

Teacher: Who can help resolve this problem? Or let me ask, how can we best define national character or the character of any nation we choose to discuss?

Student: This was part of our argument yesterday in the lunchroom. Although Harri says that Americans have certain characteristics which are quite different, he also admits that some characteristics of Swedes and Americans are the same.

Another Student: Yes, and another thing, all Americans don't think in the same way. It seems to be better to talk about individual characteristics rather than national characteristics.

Teacher: How do the rest of you feel about this?

Student: I think a majority of Americans have certain attitudes and feelings about certain things in common. For example, when we talked about the industrial revolution and automobiles we decided that people today have a certain attitude toward going places. I mean most Americans have cars and have the attitude that they can go anywhere in these cars. That wasn't true with horses or in Russia where most people still don't have cars. Another thing is that we have good roads and lots of land and don't have to have passports to travel.

Teacher: Could you be more specific as to the exact attitude you're talking about?

Student: I mean an attitude of freedom—freedom to travel.

Teacher: How do the rest of you feel about this?

Student: I guess we are saying that the American character is those characteristics which most Americans have in common. I mean the majority of Americans.

Teacher: Most of you seem to agree as I look at your heads nodding approval. Let's not forget the question raised but move on for the moment to the other question. There's the bell. Next period we'll read again and then on Friday we'll continue our discussion.

Third Discussion Session

Teacher: During our last discussion session we seemed to agree that a majority of Americans have certain characteristics in common and these characteristics were given the name of American character.

A question was raised at the last class session which we did not have time to answer: How can we say that there is such a thing as the American character when Swedes have some of the same characteristics as Americans have? How can we resolve this conflict?

Student: We talked about this after our last session. Some students felt this problem means there is no such thing as the American character but others, most of the others, felt that the total list of characteristics is the American character. I mean an American and Swede may have some characteristics in common and some not in common but it is the complete list which creates the American character or the Swedish character.

Teacher: How do the rest of you feel about this?

Student: I guess that makes sense.

Teacher: Let's not close this question but move on to any other comments you have.

Student: I talked to my dad about the American character. He's a sociologist at the university, you know. He said that he has more in common with a university professor in the Soviet Union than he has in common with most Americans. That is, his occupation, not his nation, determines his way of looking at life.

Another Student: I don't agree that your dad has more in common with a Russian professor than with most other Americans. Just look at the matter of language. He speaks English; the Russian doesn't. Your dad has a certain feeling toward his country's geography; the Russian professor has a certain feeling toward his country's geography.

The dialogue continues with no consensus as to which point of view is most acceptable.

The preceding class discussions occurred during the first week of a six-week session. It becomes immediately apparent in reading the first week's dialogue that both the teacher and his students were constantly reevaluating their own ideas as well as the ideas of others in the class. It is also interesting to note that the dialogue did not end in the classroom; it occurred during the lunch hour, at home with the family, and possibly with other acquaintances of the students and teacher. It was revealed at a teacher-parent night that many of the paperback books assigned to the students were read by their parents and formed the basis for family dialogue. One family discussion which came to the attention of the teacher was between a father and his son: the father felt that Brogan's book, *The American Character,* was too "slick" or smooth so that the reader did not question the author's ideas, but his son argued that it was refreshing to read a well written book—the result being that the reader was inspired to read other books which in turn questioned Brogan's ideas. This kind of serious dialogue between high school students and interested adults is most encouraging.[11] Do such discussions occur with textbooks rather than paperbacks? The writer doubts it![12]

Margaret Mead has suggested that it is useful to divide the study of national character into a series of steps:

1. Developing initial hypotheses
2. Subjecting these hypotheses to systematic scrutiny in the light of selected bodies of materials
3. Determining by extensive sampling techniques the prevalence and incidence of the behavior which has been identified
4. Validating the findings through prediction and experiment[13]

In the preceding classroom dialogue the reader could see steps one, two, three, and four employed, although in a far less sophisticated way than that adopted by most social scientists who deal with the concept of national character. For example, instead of sophisticated sampling techniques and statistical research methods, the students relied more on dialogue with each other and their adult acquaintances. The possibilities of introducing the students to elementary research methods of the social sciences are unlimited. For example, the students might pursue the question: "How would a political scientist operate in trying to test his hypotheses or how would a sociologist pursue the problem at hand?" Students could learn to build a questionnaire and employ interviewing techniques. Failure to use these research techniques in the following examples was due to the teacher's lack of knowledge about such matters. Public opinion polls are increasingly becoming a part of our lives; by employing similar methods, students would learn by first hand experience how such polls are taken.

The concept of national character may be used in four main ways in the social studies curriculum: (1) as the basis for the entire secondary social studies curriculum so that each course would be based on the study of national character; (2) as the basis for a particular course in the social studies curriculum such as American history; (3) as a basis for a unit within a course in the social studies curriculum; and (4) as a concept to be dealt with on an occasional basis, usually in a spontaneous way.

[11]In 1932, George S. Counts wrote: "Perhaps one of the greatest tragedies of contemporary society lies in the fact that the child is becoming increasingly isolated from the serious activities of adults." George S. Counts, *Dare the School Build a New Social Order?* (New York: The John Day Company, Inc., 1932), p. 17.

[12]For a discussion of the limitations of social studies textbooks in the United States, see *Social Studies in the United States: A Critical Appraisal,* C. Benjamin Cox and Byron G. Massialas, eds. (New York: Harcourt, Brace & World, Inc., 1967).

[13]Margaret Mead, "National Character," in Alfred L. Kroeber ed., *Anthropology Today* (Chicago: University of Chicago Press, 1959), p. 416.

Problems and Prospects

One main problem with the concept of national character is that empirical research in the area is anything but definitive and research methods are constantly being challenged. For example, the Rorschach Ink-Blot test, formerly thought to be of value in studying national character, has seriously come into question as a research instrument in studying group traits. Students in social studies classes should recognize the tentativeness of research efforts into the study of national character; they should also understand that their findings are proximate conclusions or hypotheses rather than final answers. If such an understanding is reached, it is the writer's opinion that the critical inquiry entailed in the study of national character in social studies classes will outweigh possible problems which may arise.

The study of national character may be considered by some scholars to be dysfunctional; that is, it is a waste of time to pursue this concept in social studies classes for there are more important subjects and approaches around which social studies should revolve. Those who advocate a scholarly appraisal of national character are aware of the preceding criticism. David Potter, for example, warns us that traits listed can become a "cabinet of curiosities" torn out of context for amusement purposes. The concept of national character can become a romantic notion which, in fact, becomes a chauvinistic tool. Scholars who prize objectivity are especially leery of such excessive nationalism.

The argument that the study of national character supports chauvinistic ventures is easily answered; in the hands of a chauvinist any concept employed in the teaching of social studies may be bastardized. The uses of history demonstrate this. However, in a classroom which fosters inquiry the concept of national character may be a most useful teaching and learning device.

The argument that the study of national character is dysfunctional or a waste of time is more difficult to answer in the light of the lack of research evidence to measure its worth in different social studies classes. However, the value of the concept of national character in social studies classes obviously depends on the objectives one holds for the social studies; if the teacher wants to foster inquiry and generate interest in the social studies, the concept of national character may prove to be useful; if the teacher feels that other objectives, such as subject-matter coverage, are more important, then the concept of national character may be dysfunctional for him.

A problem similar to the preceding one relates to the students' sources of information. Information, whether from informants or written sources, can be limited if not misleading. To take Mrs. Trollope's writings at face value would be humorous as well as fallacious; to read her *Domestic Manners of the Americans* in the broader context of her experiences in the United States would be both interesting and valuable. To read Alexis de Tocqueville's *Democracy in America* without realizing, as D. W. Brogan has so aptly stated, that he spent too much time with the "nice" people, would also be misleading. However, one important value in studying national character is that students would learn in an enjoyable way to question their sources of information.

Students may worship the category of national character to the exclusion of a more sophisticated analysis of mankind. That is, they may not realize that the chief value of the concept is that it is a tool of investigation. They may develop what some scholars have called a "hardening of the categories." A more optimistic view is that students might learn through the study of national character that the things about them are very complex, and proximate rather than definitive answers are usually the result of serious inquiry. In many situations students may simply conclude that X conclusion is inadequate. (It should be added that the writer does not consider the concept of national character to be the only organizing concept which may be heuristically valuable; other concepts may be of equal or greater value in various situations. But it is hoped that this chapter will inspire some uses of the concept of national character in various classroom situations—the results of which will be subject to empirical investigation.)

A related problem consists of students' efforts to establish cause-effect relationships in dealing with national character. First efforts are often quite gross but may act as general hypotheses subject to further inquiry. For example, in a world history class the students were discussing the importance of Lenin's ideas in the forming of the Soviet national character. One student contended that the ideas of pre-Bolshevik revolutionists Sergei Nechaiev and Peter Tkachev caused Lenin to assert that the anti-tsarist revolution must be in the hands of a small revolutionary elite; a second student disagreed, saying that their ideas were the same but Lenin may have had such ideas before he read Nechaiev and Tkachev, in which case their ideas simply supported his earlier conception of revolution. This kind of discussion concerning cause and effect is in the best tradition of inquiry.

A special problem exists in using the concept of national character in world history classes. Some countries are so newly formed that it might be argued that a national character has not emerged. Indonesia is a case in point. It might, however, be valuable to study how the leaders of the country have tried to make their people more nation conscious, for example, in supporting the use of one common language.

In sum, the concept of national character may prove to be too deterministic in the hands of some teachers who are more interested in consensus than in inquiry; however, this concept may be in the best tradition of inquiry when used by other social studies teachers. The advantage of using the concept of national character as an organizing concept which fosters inquiry may be seen in the dialogue in this chapter. For example, students not only questioned the concept of national character, which should be questioned in all cases in which it is used, but also questioned other concepts generated in the discussion; the concept of human nature was a case in point.

Students may also use the concept of national character to discuss the consistency or lack of consistency between a nation's ideals, its inhabitants' attitudes, and their actions.

A final advantage in using the concept of national character is that it draws upon both history and the social sciences. Most history—that is, written history—is political history, and as Mark Krug has so aptly stated, "Political history is basically national history. . . ."[14]

Conclusion

The ferment in social studies education has prompted a great deal of dialogue as to which directions the social studies should take. The traditional place which history has held in the social studies curriculum is increasingly being questioned and it is recognized that the social sciences, especially the behavioral sciences, may make an invaluable contribution to the social studies. What kinds of relationships, if any, will be developed between history and the social sciences will determine in large measure the future of the social studies. Experimental efforts along both multidisciplinary and interdisciplinary lines will have to be researched in a variety of classroom situations; at the present time we should recognize that our prescriptions are based more on hunches than on solid research findings. It is the writer's feeling that interdisciplinary efforts will be more fruitful than multidisciplinary efforts because of the eclectic orientation of the social studies. This chapter has described one avenue of innovation which may properly be labeled interdisciplinary. The writer's thesis is that organizing concepts may be useful to social studies students; the particular concept cited in this chapter is that of national character. It is hoped that more sophisticated efforts to employ the concept of national character in social studies classes will be stimulated by the ideas in this chapter.

Annotated Bibliography

Brogan, D. W., *The American Character.* Vintage Books, New York, 1959. This classic work was written by a Scotsman whose sympathy for the great American experiment is readily apparent in his writings. Brogan argues that there is an interrelation between the paradoxes in American political system and the American character.

[14]Mark M. Krug, *History and the Social Sciences,* (Waltham, Mass.: Blaisdell Publishing Co., Inc., 1967), p. 14.

_____ and Verney, Douglas V., *Political Patterns in Today's World.* Harcourt, Brace & World, Inc., New York, 1963. A brief, comparative introduction to political science based on comparing American government to other liberal-democracies and other government systems. Liberal democracies compared are the United States, the United Kingdom, France, and Sweden. Liberal democracies are then contrasted to the communist world.

Brown, Ralph A., and Brown, Marian R. (eds.), *Impressions of America.* Harcourt, Brace & World, New York, 1966. A two volume compilation of the writings of foreign visitors who came to observe the New World. This collection was especially edited for secondary social studies classes. It may be extremely valuable in implementing some of the ideas in the previous chapter on the study of national character.

Cogley, John (ed.), *The American Character.* The Center for the Study of Democratic Institutions, Santa Barbara, Calif., 1962. This little book presents excerpts from speeches and discussions on the subject of the American character held in 1961. Well known speakers, such as Henry Steele Commager and William O. Douglas contributed to the conference.

Commager, Henry Steele (ed.), *America in Perspective.* The New American Library, New York, 1961. Commager's Introduction seeks the permanent rather than the transcient in the American character as observed by the authors of the chapters in this book (from Crèvecoeur to Brogan).

Duijker, H.C.J., and Frijda, N.H., *National Character and National Stereotypes.* North-Holland Publishing Company, Amsterdam, The Netherlands, 1960. The most definitive single volume on the study of national character. Efforts to deal with the concept of national character are reviewed and there is an excellent bibliography. This report was prepared for the International Union of Scientific Psychology and published by the International Committee for Social Sciences Documentation.

Inkeles, Alex, "National Character and Modern Political Systems," in Francis L.K. Hsu (ed.), *Psychological Anthropology.* Dorsey Press, Homewood, Ill., 1961, pp. 172-208. The author advocates recognizing politics and national character as highly differentiated systems of variables; failure to make such a distinction in national character research studies is documented by the author. A comparative social psychology of the political process is needed, according to the author, to supplement our traditional study of politics.

Laski, Harold J., *The American Democracy.* The Viking Press, New York, 1948. The following characteristics of the American spirit are listed by Laski:

future-looking, dynamism, worship of bigness, sense of destiny, fluidity of classes, pioneer spirit, individualism, antistatism, versality, empiricism and the priority of the practical, zeal for careers and wealth, self-help and self-interest, gospel of hard work, and sense of property.

Linton, Ralph, "The Concept of National Character," in Alfred H. Stanton and Stewart E. Perry (eds.), *Personality and Political Crisis.* Free Press of Glencoe, Inc., New York, 1951, pp. 133-150. The author cites the problems involved in scientific study of nations rather than that of smaller social groups. Various research techniques are discussed in the process.

Mead, Margaret, "National Character," in Alfred L. Kroeber (ed.), *Anthropology Today.* University of Chicago Press, Chicago, 1953, pp. 396-421. A review of attempts to deal with the concept of national character and a discussion of the assumptions on which national character research has been conducted. Also a discussion of the unique contribution which the anthropological approach to the study of contemporary culture makes in studying complex societies.
_____ "The Study of National Character," in Daniel Lerner and Harold D. Lasswell (eds.), *The Policy Sciences: Recent Developments in Scope and Method.* Stanford University Press, Stanford, California, 1951, pp. 70-85. The first part of this chapter deals with the evolution of research into national character; the second part discusses the diverse methods used in the study of national character.

Hsu, Francis L. K., "American Core Value and National Character," in Francis L. K. Hsu (ed.), *Psychological Anthropology.* Dorsey Press, Homewood, Ill., 1961, pp. 209-230. Difficulties and contradictions involved in national character studies are cited; the author especially blames Western and American scholars for their enthnocentrism.

Lerner, Max, *America as a Civilization.* Simon and Schuster, New York, 1961. This two volume work has in the author's words attempted to grasp " . . .the pattern and inner meaning of contemporary American civilization and its relation to the world of today." Chapter eleven entitled "The Idea of American Civilization" has a section (pages 67-71) on the subject of national character. The author's thesis is that national character ". . . is best sought at the point where cultural norms in America shape personality and character, and where in turn the human material and the energies of Americans leave their impact on the fabric of the culture." Page 69.

Myrdal, Gunnar, *An American Dilemma.* Harper & Row, Publishers, New York, 1944. A discussion of the Negro in America and modern democracy.

Niebuhr, Reinhold, and Heimert, Alan, *A Nation So Conceived*. Charles Scribner's Sons, New York, 1963. This book was prepared for the Center for the Study of Democratic Institutions in connection with its Study of the American Character. National character is defined in the first chapter as a pattern of consistent behavior, created on the one hand by an original ethnic, geographic and cultural endowment, and on the other hand by the vicissitudes of history, which shape and reshape, purify, corrupt, and transmute this endowment. The quest for national identity is developed as we moved from an agrarian society to an industrial society.

Platt, Washington, *National Character in Action*. Rutgers University Press, New Brunswick, N.J., 1961. The author is interested in the practical applications of the concept of national character to problems of foreign intelligence and to foreign nations. He argues that there are two meanings of national character. Examples are: traits of character predominant in a large number of American individuals; and the character of a nation in dealing with other nations. The two meanings are sometimes in conflict so that the latter does not necessarily reflect the former.

Potter, David M., *People of Plenty*. University of Chicago Press, Chicago, 1954. Part I traces the history of the use of the concept of national character; Part II deals with a particular theme, abundance, and its part in the shaping of American character. The author's attempt to employ the behavioral sciences in his study make this book unique among national character studies by historians.

Williams, Robin M., Jr., *American Society*. Alfred A. Knopf, Inc., New York, 1951. The author lists fifteen "major value orientations": stress on achievement and success; stress on activity and work; a tendency to see the world in moral terms; humanitarianism; stress on efficiency and practicality; belief in progress; valuing of material comfort; avowal and (to an extent) practice of equality; avowal and practice of freedom; emphasis on external conformity; belief in science and in secular rationality; stress on nationalism and patriotism; stress on democracy; cult of the individual personality, and its value and dignity; and belief in racism and group superiority.

Index